SKYE
THE·ISLAND

words
JAMES HUNTER

photographs
CAILEAN MACLEAN

MAINSTREAM PUBLISHING

First published in 1986 by
MAINSTREAM PUBLISHING COMPANY (EDINBURGH), LTD.
7 Albany Street
Edinburgh EH1 3UG

British Library Cataloguing in Publication Data
Hunter, James, *1937-*
    Skye : the island.
    1. Skye——Social life and customs
    I. Title
    941.1'82   DA880.S6

    ISBN 1-85158-017-4

The publishers gratefully acknowledge financial assistance from the
Scottish Arts Council in the publication of this volume.

Typeset in 11 point Andover by Mainstream Publishing.
Printed by Collins, Great Britain.

To the people of the island

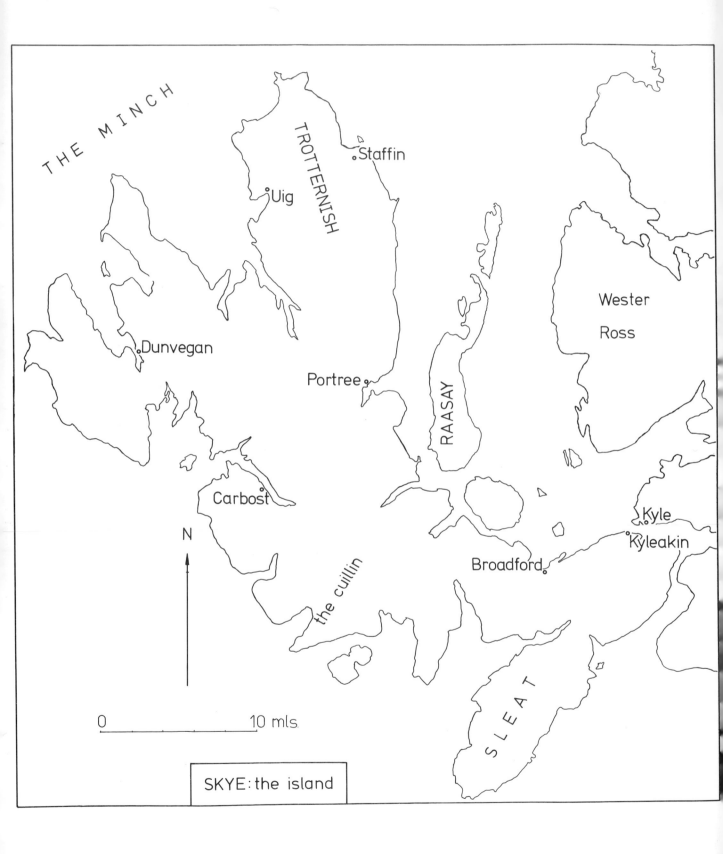

THE MINCH

TROTTERNISH

Staffin

Uig

Dunvegan

Portree

Wester Ross

RAASAY

Carbost

Kyle

Kyleakin

N

the cuillin

Broadford

0   10 mls.

SLEAT

SKYE: the island

'S nuair bhios mise 's na bordaibh
Bidh mo chomhradh mar fhaistneachd,

'S pillidh gineal na tuatha
Rinneadh fhuadach thar saile.

'S bidh na baigearan uasal
Air an ruaig mar bha iadsan;

Feidh is caoraich 'gan cuibhleadh
'S bidh na glinn air an aiteach;

Am cur is am buana
'S am duais do na meairlich;

'S theid na tobhtachan fuara
Thogail suas le ar cairdean.

Mairi Mhor nan Oran.

1

IN Gaelic, the language of its people for most of the last 2000 years, Skye is *an t-eilean Sgiathanach*. Often it is simply *an t-eilean*, the island. *Tha mi a dol do 'n eilean*, a Skye person might say in Glasgow or some other place of exile: I am going to the island. And today that is my purpose also. From Kyle of Lochalsh I look across to Skye, its hilly outline blurred by a fine drizzle. *Tha mise cuideachd a dol do 'n eilean*. I, too, am going to the island.

*   *   *

The island is reached, at Kyleakin, with an unceremonious clang of steel on concrete and a slightly nervous revving of car engines. The ferry traffic departs hurriedly along a road that boasts more double yellow lining than most city streets. At the top of the concrete slipway, beside a jumbled pile of lobster creels, half a dozen herring gulls are quarrelling intermittently about the ownership of a piece of refuse. There are few other signs of activity. It is mid-afternoon in what is still the tourist season and any commercial opportunity missed now will not come round again until next spring. But the Isle of Skye Ice Cream Factory, a couple of hundred yards from the ferry terminal, has a *closed* sign hanging, a little defeatedly, in its rain-streaked window. On a day like this, I suppose, there is not much demand for cooling refreshments.

On the eastern side of Kyleakin is a little inlet, not so much a harbour as an anchorage, where the outgoing tide has left two or three boats on their sides among a lot of gleaming orange seaweed. Beyond the inlet is a row of snow-white houses. And beyond them, maybe half a kilometre from the village, is Castle Moil. Once it guarded the strategically important passage between Loch Alsh and the Inner Sound. Now its walls are so reduced by wind and water as to give it the appearance of an extracted and upturned molar in an advanced state of decay.

With the now heavier rain rattling incessantly on my anorak, I make my way towards the castle by way of a muddy path and a muddier beach. The pointed knoll on which the ruin sits, its earth sweetened, no doubt, by lime from the crumbling ramparts overhead, is noticeably grassier than the peaty hillsides all around. From it I watch the ferry load, unload, leave and return. And I try to imagine how Kyleakin would have looked more than 150 years ago when a woman called Christian Watt was one of the island's regular visitors.

Christian was no tourist. Holidaymaking, in the middle of the nineteenth century, was a rich person's pastime. And Christian was not rich. She came to Skye because men and boats from the Aberdeenshire port of Fraserburgh, to which she belonged, were then opening up a commercial herring fishery in the Minch — that wide stretch of windswept water between Skye and the Western Isles. Fishing, of course, was an exclusively male occupation. But where there were herring to be caught there was also work for the women who split, cleaned and salted the fish before packing them into kegs and barrels that would afterwards be shipped across the North Sea to Germany and Russia.

Christian was a herring gutter. And to be a gutter, as can be learned from island women who followed the same trade as recently as the 1940s, was not to make an easy living. When your fingers have been cut and hacked repeatedly by a slimy gutting knife, when the resulting gashes have not had time to heal and when you are obliged, each morning, to plunge your hands once more into the brine used to preserve and cure the herring you are handling — well, then, you weep for half an hour or more, they say, until a growing numbness provides its own rough and ready anaesthetic.

A woman who leaves home to take up that type of employment, perhaps, has to be more than normally self-resiliant. Christian, at any rate, was sufficiently independent minded to set little store on the respectful attitude expected of her by those who occupied places far above her own in the elaborately graded pecking order which supplied Victorian Britain with a handy means of categorising their fellow citizens in terms of wealth, rank, title and position. Christian Watt's name was close to the bottom of that particular listing. The name of Godfrey, Lord Macdonald, owner of the greater part of Skye, was very near the top. For them to have met was unusual. For her to have abused him publicly — in the robust and raucous Scots of her native Fraserburgh — was quite extraordinary.

Their encounter, or confrontation, took place on the jetty here at Kyleakin one day in the 1850s. Lord Macdonald, Christian remembered afterwards, 'had a party of toffs with him'. And one can picture still these toffs; their tweeds; their dogs; their waiting carriages; their discernible air of being in complete charge of their own and others' destiny. Skye people, if there were any about, would have been keeping out of this group's way; certainly doing nothing to attract their attention. Christian, however, exercised no such discretion. Well aware that her conduct would be all the more embarrassing to Lord Macdonald because of his being surrounded by other members of the gentry, she proceeded to harangue this 'greedy character', as she had called him, about the many evictions which were then taking place on his land. 'I said to him before his audience,' she recalled. '"You are lower than the outscourings of any pigsty."' And had he been dealing with Aberdeenshire folk

Churchyard, Cillchrist, Strathaird.

instead of Skye's more easily intimidated inhabitants, Christian assured the island's principal proprietor, 'his fine castle would have been burned down'.

Lord Macdonald's response is not recorded. He must have been surprised, annoyed, even angered. And Christian, though she did not say so when recounting her adventure, would surely have been hustled speedily away.

But was that the end of the matter? Did Lord Macdonald feel his public humiliation to have been in any way deserved? Did he, in fact, think himself guilty of the crimes Christian had attributed to him? Perhaps to some extent, he did; for, by his more intimate friends at all events, Lord Macdonald was believed to be, at bottom, a humane man. As such, or so it was claimed, he was greatly saddened, in later life at least, by the innumerable cruelties which had been perpetrated in his name. And well he might have been. The men who managed the Macdonald estates on his behalf, after all, had made hundreds of families homeless. And among these families were many who were well known to the Fraserburgh fisher lassie, Christian Watt.

One of Christian's evicted friends was called Kate MacLeod; a girl who had brought the Aberdeenshire herring gutters their daily supply of milk; a girl to whom they had given bits and pieces of clothing; a girl from whom Christian had learned a word or two of Gaelic. On the morning after my arrival in Skye I went to see the place where she once lived.

The track to Kate MacLeod's former home begins at a stony bay called Camas Malag on the eastern shore of Loch Slapin. From there the way lies southward across a series of rounded ridges sloping smoothly towards the sea. And, as always in this watery terrain, the diminutive glen between each pair of ridges contains its own well-filled burn. The largest of these, certainly the noisiest, is Allt nan Leac. Beside it are half a dozen ash trees which the stream's rocky gorge has protected from the all-devouring sheep. These trees, like the odd clump of flowering heather beside the path, add some badly needed colour to the late summer landscape.

Late summer, I said. And in fact it is only the third day of September. But weeks of seemingly incessant rain have already bleached and flattened the deer grass. The bracken is already taking on its autumn shading. And under a slate grey sky, the open ocean beyond the junction of Loch Slapin and Loch Eishort has a black and stormy look.

The early morning weather forecast promised that the first snow of winter would fall on the high tops before the day is out. That is perfectly believable. The gusty wind is from the north or the north-east and the occasional spatters of rain have a hard and sleety feel to them.

Beyond Allt nan Leac the gravelled track zig-zags steeply upwards. Then it descends again and turns sharply to the east. Suddenly and quite unexpectedly, you are walking through green fields. And all around are the remains of houses. The sites of some are indicated now by little more than angular undulations in the turf. Others are better preserved, their walls four or five feet high, their stonework still in reasonable shape. One of these ruins, there is no knowing which, was home to Kate MacLeod on whose behalf Christian Watt launched that stinging attack on Godfrey William, Lord Macdonald.

The ordnance survey map I carry in my pocket gives the place the name by which Kate MacLeod and Christian Watt knew it: Suisnish. Its land, by Skye standards, is good; much better, for example, than that available to still occupied townships like Ord and Tokavaig on the opposite side of Loch Eishort. But Suisnish nevertheless ceased to exist as a crofting community in the early 1850s when its tenants were ordered to quit both their holdings and their homes. And in seeking to excuse the ensuing evictions, one of Lord Macdonald's agents was to invent the least plausible reason ever given for such an obviously harsh and heartless course of action. In instructing that the Suisnish people be removed, said this particular propagandist, Lord Macdonald have been 'prompted by motives of benevolance, piety and humanity'. What his critics had failed to grasp, you see, was that Lord Macdonald had been 'prompted by motives of benevolence, piety and humanity'. What his critics had failed to grasp, you see, was that Lord Macdonald's Suisnish tenants had been ejected simply 'because they were too

Well aware that their laird was more interested in their land than in their religious welfare, the Suisnish crofters fought the constables sent to remove them. That delayed their expulsion. It did not prevent it. Soon Suisnish, like so many similar localities, had been converted into a sheep farm and most of its

Loch Strathaird.

people, Kate MacLeod among them, had been shipped off to the Australian and Canadian colonies.

They went in the reluctant manner of all the world's dispossessed before and since. On the afternoon of their going there happened to be at work on one of the hills above Strath Suardal, through which they had to pass to reach Broadford Bay and the waiting emigrant ships, a young geologist called Archibald Geikie. More than half a century later, as an old man, he was to write about his still vivid recollections of the scenes he had witnessed that day in Skye.

'There were old men and women, too feeble to walk, who were placed in carts,' he began. 'The younger members of the community, on foot, were carrying their bundles of clothes and household effects, while their children, with looks of alarm, walked alongside.' Many of the refugees were weeping. And when the 'long and motley procession', as Geikie described it, reached Kilbride, a mile or so to the east of Camas Malag, 'a cry of grief', in the geologist's words, 'went up to heaven'. To the young man on the hillside, indeed, that 'plaintive wail' seemed to encapsulate the tragedy he was observing. Even when the departing families had pressed on slowly and reluctantly towards Loch Cill Chriosd and Broadford, he recalled, 'the sound seemed to re-echo through the whole wide valley of Strath in one prolonged note of desolation'.

At Kilbride, on the cold, raw day I walked to Suisnish, I called on Walter MacIntyre, a crofter and retired merchant seaman. Walter's grandmother was born in Suisnish. 'That would have been around 1850,' he says, 'just about the time the place was cleared.' There were some two dozen families in Suisnish then, Walter thinks. But his own people were not among those forcibly removed. His grandmother's father, his own great-grandfather that would be, was lucky enough to get a job on an estate other than Lord Macdonald's. And eventually he was able to settle, with his children, on the croft which Walter still occupies.

Before her marriage, Walter's grandmother was Anne MacInnes. The common names in Suisnish, he says, were MacInnes and MacRae. Why that should have been the case puzzles him a little. These are unusual names to find in Skye, an island of MacDonalds and MacLeods, Nicolsons and MacKinnons. But in both Suisnish and Boreraig, a neighbouring village cleared at the same time, people called MacRae and MacInnes were in the majority. And they had been so, Walter believes, for at least two centuries.

He is not the only Skye person who can claim a family connection with Suisnish, Walter MacIntyre makes clear, naming a number of others. But not many Suisnish people remained on the island as far as he knows. For the most part they went to Australia, Walter has heard; to the Hunter River district of New South Wales, he thinks.

And what of those families who went overseas? Has anything ever been heard of them? Not recently, Walter says. But about 70 years ago, during the First World War, two strangers called one morning at a house here in Kilbride. They were in military uniform, the story goes, and, while there was nothing particularly noteworthy in that at the time, these two young men clearly did not belong to any Highland regiment. Their uniforms, in fact, were those of the Australian and New Zealand Army Corps. They were on leave, they explained, and they wanted to be directed to Suisnish and Boreraig so that they could see the spot where their people had come from.

These soldiers were, perhaps, the grandsons of Suisnish or Boreraig crofters. If they survived repeated tours of duty on the Western Front and went home and married, their own grandchildren will now be men and women in their thirties and forties. They, too, may have families of their own. And since few of us know very much, if anything, about our great-great-great grandparents, the younger generation of people descended from the Suisnish emigrants — and living now in Sydney, Melbourne, Brisbane, Montreal, Toronto, Winnipeg, Vancouver or any one of a thousand other places — are almost certainly unaware of how they came to be where they are.

Suppose, I think, while sheltering from the strengthening wind in one of Suisnish's many tumbledown cottages; suppose it were possible to trace some of these people and bring them here. Would they wish that things had turned out differently? Would they feel, on looking at these once cultivated slopes on this high, blunt promontory between Loch Slapin and Loch Eishort, that they ought to be occupying this place and growing crops and raising stock as at least some of their contemporaries are doing in other parts of the island? Or would

Walter MacIntyre.

they believe themselves well out of Skye and be glad to be well away from Suisnish? And if, most tantalisingly of all, they were to give an affirmative answer to that last question, something which seems more than likely, would that prove that the deportation of the original inhabitants of localities like this was, after all, the best fate that could have befallen them?

There are those who argue that such is the case; those who say that, by removing them and transporting them abroad, last century's landlords did their tenants something of a favour. I have never been convinced by any such line of reasoning. Among the victims of the clearances, I admit, were many individuals who — having survived their eviction and, more problematically, the ocean passage which followed it — made good use of the opportunities available to them in their new countries. And it is equally true, I agree, that Australians, New Zealanders, Canadians and Americans called MacLeod, MacDònald or, for that matter, MacRae or MacInnes, are generally better off today than their namesakes here in Skye. But to conclude that this circumstance somehow excuses the conduct of men like the fourth Lord Macdonald and his representatives seems to me to be as unimaginative, insensitive and insulting as to maintain that, because American blacks have higher living standards than West Africans, the slave trade was a very good thing.

As Christian Watt recognised long ago, there can be no justification for what was done at Suisnish. Nor can Skye be understood without some appreciation of the emotions aroused by such a place. That is why, if I were to be asked for directions by any of the many overseas visitors who come to the island in search of their origins, I should be tempted to turn them away from the castles and the mansions made so much of by the tourist brochures. Instead, I should point out to them, in the way that it was pointed out to those ANZAC soldiers mentioned by Walter MacIntyre, the rough and gravelly track that starts at Camas Malag.

*   *   *

At Broadford the mist clings clammily to the Forestry Commission plantations on Cnoc na Cachaileith. The river is in spate and the cyclists making their way to the youth hostel at the north end of the bay are wearing yellow capes. If Portree is the London of Skye, said one nineteenth-century visitor to the island, Broadford is its Manchester; the place where, as in that other grimier shrine of commerce, goods were sold and deals done. But Broadford's harbour is no longer in the import-export business. And the village, like so many other island communities, is primarily a stopping-off point on the tourist circuit. This summer, in the wet, the tourists are not well pleased. The glass on the seaward side of the telephone box at the Broadford information centre has been smashed and replaced by a sheet of damp-edged hardboard. On it is this caustic scribble: *Carole, Christophe, Eddy, Francois, Franck, Sylvan sont passes ici a 12h 42m – 13/7/85 – et il pleut comme d'habitude.* Mentally, I translate that last phrase as: it rains habitually. It is not quite idiomatic. But today it seems like a good motto.

'It's the wind I notice most of all,' an islander remarks when I complain about the weather. 'People talk a lot about the rain and, well, yes it's a nuisance, right enough. But you can dress to keep dry. And you can dress to keep warm. From the wind, though, there's no escape. On winter mornings, going out to feed the cattle, I've had to turn my back to it to be able to breathe. I've seen it carry away almost everything that wasn't tied down. And I've lain awake for hours at night while it's whistled and shrieked round the house. It's easy to hate the wind in Skye.'

Certainly there are few days without wind on the island. And as well as its strength, its direction is important; for each wind — north, east, south and west — brings its own distinctive brand of weather. 'The wind's shifting a bit,' people say anxiously on a good day and hopefully on a bad one; for such movement is an almost unfailing harbinger of a switch from one set of weather conditions to another.

Southerly and south-westerly winds, which blow more regularly than any others, come laden with moisture drawn up from the Atlantic. They swathe the hills in the mist and cloud which are so characteristic of the West Highland climate. And though wet weather can reach the island from any point on the compass, Skye's frequent and lengthy spells of drenching rain are firmly linked with these prevailing south-south-westerlies.

As the wind veers from south-west into north-west, the steady rain gives way to showers. These, however, are not the benign dampenings of the south

Fisherman's shed.

country. They are face-stinging downpours which, in winter and early spring, regularly turn to hail or even snow. In north-westerly weather, at any time between November and April, a watery sun will be ceaselessly eclipsed by huge piles of cloud pushing ponderously eastward from the Minch. At their base these clouds are inky black. And between them and the equally sombre sea there hangs the ragged grey curtain of sleety snow which will quickly be drawn across the entire landscape.

Breezes reaching the island from a generally northerly or north-easterly direction provide Skye with its best weather. In winter these winds, which emanate from the Arctic, are likely to be cold; even in summer they may well be on the cool side. But at all times of the year they sweep away the cloud and bring perfect visibility. In May and June, when such winds are not uncommon, there are often several days and, on rarer occasions, even several weeks of practically unbroken sunshine. And especially in the late evening, when the slightly yellowish westerly light lingers on the newly grass grown hillsides, every boulder, every stone, every deer and every grazing sheep can be picked out from further away than one would have believed possible.

Easterlies and south-easterlies, too, are generally to be welcomed. In winter, mind you, they can impose a bitter, black frost which solidifies the peat bogs and gives an icy rim to even the fastest flowing hill burn. But in summer they bring the island its warmest weather. In July and August, in a good season, an easterly air will leave the heather dry and crackling below your boots; the tar will bubble stickily on the roads; rivers will be no more than barely connected chains of pools in wide beds of gravel; and the steadily thickening heat haze will eventually reduce the Cuillins to a set of blue-tinged shadows.

* * *

At Luib, a few kilometres beyond Broadford on the Portree road, one of Skye's few remaining black houses has been converted into a folk museum. There are a number of these institutions on the island now. And I suppose, being undeniably interested in what has gone before, I should find such places a greater attraction than I do. But people have always seemed to me to matter more than things. And the survival of community and culture and language is of infinitely greater importance, to my mind, than the preservation of wooden ploughs and chairs and spinning wheels. Though I pay my entrance fee and spend a minute or two in each of the Luib museum's neatly maintained rooms, the assembled artefacts remain just that: objects. There is not here, as far as I am concerned anyway, that sense of contact with the island's past which is obtainable at Suisnish.

There has been recently a tendency to romanticise the black house. And there is, in consequence, no lack of lamentation about the supposedly good old days when folk sat cosily under its thatch, warming themselves at its peat fire and dining on salt herring and oatcakes instead of polythene-wrapped bacon and factory-baked bread.

In fact, the black house of a century or so ago was a grim and unprepossessing dwelling. Its walls were perpetually damp. It had no windows and no chimney, the smoke from the fire which burned perpetually in one corner being left to find its way out through a hole in the roof. The floor was trampled mud; the furniture virtually non-existent.

The crofter's cattle lived under the same straw-thatched, leaking roof as the crofter and his family. Beasts and humans entered by the same door. Between byre and kitchen there was often no partition and, particularly in winter, when the cattle had to be kept inside for weeks at a stretch, dung and filth penetrated to practically every corner of the building.

In these dark, dank, insanitary and foul-smelling homes, typhoid and cholera persisted long after they had been eradicated in many other parts of Britain. And that most dreaded of island diseases, tuberculosis, haunted the black house well into the present century. From all such illnesses, children suffered most severely. And the now prevalent notion that the barefooted boys and girls reared in such habitations were especially happy and contented, I am afraid, is just so much nostalgic imagining.

The reality is to be glimpsed in this 1877 account of a visit made to Torrin, the township adjacent to Kilbride where Walter MacIntyre now lives. The writer came from Edinburgh which itself contained some notorious slums. But Torrin clearly bore unfavourable comparison with the very worst of these: 'At the top of the village, gathered in a listless way on a bit of moss land before an almost ruinous cottage, were a dozen children — as squalid and as miserable as any that could be produced from the innermost dens of the Cowgate. What I saw there at Torrin, I have seen at many places since. Children — not the bronzed, healthy urchins such as one meets in Lowland country districts — but puny, uncombed, blear-eyed, shivering little objects. This sorrowful index to the condition of the crofter forces itself very strongly on a stranger's notice as he passes through this island.'

The people who lived in such conditions, of course, did not do so willingly. Their landlords, however, had imposed on them a system which made it inevitable that bad housing would be all but universal. The key to that system was an all-embracing insecurity which ensured that, should a man be tempted to build himself a superior house, his rent would be increased automatically to take account of his holding's enhanced value. Indeed, he might well be evicted if his landlord, his landlord's factor or some other hanger-on happened to be looking for a better than average croft for someone to whom the estate management owed a favour. Such occurrences were common and they acted as a powerful disincentive to improvements of any kind.

The solution, suggested repeatedly by outside observers as well as by islanders themselves, was to give crofters security of tenure. When that happened, new, more attractive and healthier homes soon appeared on most crofts. But the bringing about of that long overdue transformation, which island landowners had their own good reasons for opposing, required a virtual revolution; a revolution which began a little further up Skye's eastern coast, at a place called Braes.

Skye (white strip) start an attack on the Kincraig goal. King George V playing field, Portree.

2

APART from an occasional buzzing of flies and the repetitive breaking of waves on the shingly beach at Camus a Mhor-bheoil, the slopes above Braes are perfectly peaceful this summer morning. From the handily squared-off boulder which I've cushioned with my temporarily redundant waterproofs, I have a wide view north to Ben Tianavaig, its distinctively layered and tilted outcrops highlighted by the sun. East lies Raasay. South is Sconser and the rounded slope of Glamaig. Both sky and sea are blue today. The air is clear and it is possible to distinguish the shapes of individual gulls squatting on the dark surface of Sgeir Dubh, a foam-ringed rock a few hundred metres offshore.

Nearer hand, several sheep, healthy looking and with this year's lambs still in tow, are moving casually about the hillside. Down below, alongside the single track road into Braes, are some scrubby hazels, birches and willows. Up here there are none. These sheep and their predecessors have seen to that. And not only has their ceaseless grazing removed all trace of trees; it has helped expose, especially in steeper spots, little drifts of sharp-edged, flinty fragments which, over the centuries, have parted company with the underlying rock.

There are any amount of these spiky stones within reach. Any one of them, I think, if impelled with sufficient force, could cut open a man's head, maybe fracture his skull. I pick one up. It fits comfortably in my hand. I throw it, as hard as I can, towards the road. It curves up, outward, down; it strikes the fence at the bottom of the hill with a sharp, metallic clang that dies away only slowly. How would I react, I wonder, if instead of bouncing off that still thrumming wire, the stone I have just thrown had smashed into the upturned face of a police constable? Had I lived in Braes a century or so ago, I know, I would have been fiercely pleased. Had I been here on this hillside on the morning of 19 April, 1882, I would have gone on to throw another stone and then another and another.

The Braes townships of Peinchorran, Balmeanach and Gedintailor are now thought to be attractive localities in which to own a home; are now described, in fact, as the island's premier residential area in the property pages of the local press. Then they were drab, sad places; their houses dilapidated, their fields exhausted, their prospects anything but favourable. 'The principal thing we have to complain of is our poverty,' said one Peinchorran crofter in the 1880s. 'The smallness of our holdings and the inferior quality of the land is what has caused our poverty; and the way in which the poor crofters are huddled together and the best part of the land devoted to deer forests and big farms.'

Among the many thousands of hectares thus set aside for sport was the high ground above Sconser on the south side of Loch Sligachan. This particular tract of territory where successive Macdonald lairds and their friends, in the manner of the Victorian gentry and aristocracy from the queen and prime minister downwards, stalked stags each August and September, had been enlarged by the simple expedient of evicting the crofters who had formerly occupied its more low-lying fringes. And those among the consequently dispossessed families who were not immediately shipped to Canada were moved to Braes where already diminutive holdings had to be subdivided further to make room for them.

The inevitable outcome was that no one had enough land and that some especially unfortunate individuals were left without any land at all. One such was John Mathieson who lived at Achnahannait, some three kilometres north of Gedintailor. 'I want to say,' he stated forecefully in 1883, 'that it is the want of land, and the dearness of it, that is leaving the people so poor. My own great-

Raasay ferry with Braes in the background.

grandfather was tenant in Achnahannait and had a fourth part of it to himself. My grandfather succeeded him and had a fifth part of Achnahannait. My father succeeded my grandfather and had an eighth part of the land; and in his lifetime he came to be reduced to a sixteenth of the land. My father had six sons, of whom I am the eldest and not one of them would get a sod from Lord Macdonald.'

Here in Braes, then, there had been for long enough no lack of animosity towards the community's Macdonald landlords and the men who served them. And in 1865 that animosity had been sharpened and intensified by the Macdonald estate management's decision to deprive the Braes crofters of their longstanding and jealously guarded right to pasture their stock on Ben Lee, the lumpy hill which lies to the west of the townships of Gedintailor, Balmeanach and Peinchorran and which effectively isolates these places from the modern main road that loops round the head of Loch Sligachan and continues through Glen Varragill towards Portree.

Ben Lee, at well under half their height, is not one of the island's more self-evident rivals to the Cuillins. In the early part of 1882, however, had you asked the average southerner to name a peak in Skye, Sgurr Alasdair and Sgurr nan Gillean would have posed no challenge whatsoever to Ben Lee; for the previously obscure issue of the Ben Lee grazings was then at the centre of an increasingly impassioned national debate and the not infrequently dramatic doings of the inhabitants of Peinchorran, Balmeanach and Gedintailor were being chronicled daily by practically every newspaper in the land.

* * *

In order to supplement the meagre earnings they derived from their crofts, the Braes men were in the habit of going annually to what they called the Kinsale fishings in the south-west of Ireland. There they sailed out of small and hospitable coastal villages in County Cork and County Kerry. And there, when they came ashore in search of a little relaxation, they mingled with villagers whose Gaelic, though not identical to their own, was similar enough in tone and texture to allow the Skyemen to converse pretty freely with their hosts. And in the summer of 1881 there was plenty to talk about in either Scots or Irish Gaelic.

For months past, Ireland had been in chaos. An organisation called the Irish Land League had been formed to campaign for a radical and arguably long overdue improvement in the condition of the country's tenant farmers and smallholders. The Land League, which had quickly attracted an enormous following, had placed at the centre of its programme a demand that all agricultural occupiers be given legally guaranteed security of tenure. In pursuit of this objective, and of others equally far reaching in their implications, the League's members had refused to pay their rents; they had intimidated and terrorised a number of landowners; they had staged a series of monster meetings or demonstrations; and they had determinedly ostracised all those individuals — such as a certain Captain Boycott whose name thus passed into the language — who were considered to be obstructing Land League progress.

All this the Braes men heard about at length, no doubt, over the glasses of whiskey they downed around their Irish friends' peat fires. All this and a good deal more: how Ireland's landlords, feared and hated for generations, had at last been taken on by Ireland's people and how the people had eventually won; how the British government in London, then in charge of all Ireland, had first responded to the Irish challenge by trying to crush the League; how prime minister William Gladstone and his cabinet had been obliged, in the end, to give way and to introduce a Parliamentary Bill which conceded much, some said most, of what the Land League had been so vociferously and so effectively requesting.

Back on their boats at the end of such a talk-filled evening, the Braes men would have lit their pipes and discussed what they had been told. Tentatively at first, then with increasing conviction, they would have related events in Ireland to their own predicament in Skye. When they got home to the island, they would have begun to assure each other, they would follow the Irish example. They, too, would stand up for their rights. They would show their landlord that they were not to be taken for granted any more.

That November, the men of Gedintailor, Balmeanach and Peinchorran

Work at the fank in North Skye.

signed a carefully worded petition which they forwarded to Lord Macdonald. It asked, quite politely, that their former pastures on Ben Lee be restored to them. This was, inevitably, refused. How Lord Macdonald disposed of his lands had absolutely nothing to do with them, it was made clear to the Braes tenants. And they had been overly presumptuous, it was made equally clear to them, in even raising such a matter with him.

A week or two later, on the Martinmas term-day, the annual rents of the Braes crofters were due for payment. But no rents were forthcoming. On the morning that they should have been handing over the guineas husbanded carefully for that purpose, the people of Peinchorran, Balmeanach and Gedintailor marched in procession to Portree, some twelve kilometres distant. There they halted outside the office of Lord Macdonald's factor, a certain Alexander MacDonald. 'Their rents,' an official account of the subsequent proceedings records them as announcing, 'would not be paid that day, or any other day, until Ben Lee was returned to them.'

To this unprecedented gesture of defiance, the sixth Lord Macdonald responded in the tried and tested manner of his predecessors. From Armadale Castle, the Macdonald family mansion in the southern part of Skye, there came orders to evict a dozen Braes crofters by way of encouraging the others to give up their insubordination. About this, it should be stressed, there was nothing at all unusual or illegal. The Braes men had not paid their rents and, having failed to do so, they had forfeited such slim claims as they possessed to the miserable plots they held as Lord Macdonald's tenants.

The necessary eviction orders, therefore, were readily obtained in the local court. And on 7 April, 1882, a sheriff-officer was dispatched from Portree to serve these orders on the men whose names were to be added to the long, long list of people forcibly removed from their homes at the instigation of successive Lords Macdonald.

On this occasion, however, things were not to go in accordance with the proprietorial plan. The Braes people had posted sentries on the hills overlooking the Portree road and the approach of the luckless sheriff-officer was duly known to everyone in the district a good half hour before his actual arrival. When he was still a kilometre or so short of his destination, he was met by a crowd of between 150 and 200 people. All of them, it was afterwards reported, were 'determined'; determined not to be intimidated by their laird; determined to use whatever force was required to prevent the hateful eviction orders reaching their intended recipients.

The sheriff-officer's name was Martin. He was also Lord Macdonald's deputy factor and, in the fashion of a time when there was thought to be no conflict of interest in serving both an island landlord and an island court of law, he was delivering in one capacity the ejection notices he had applied for in the other. But neither of his dual offices was to protect him that spring morning. He was seized and assaulted. His impressive-looking legal documents were wrenched roughly from his grasp and to the accompaniment of mingled cheers and jeers, they were burned ceremonially before him.

Prior to this incident, the Braes people's quarrel with Lord Macdonald had

Talisker Bay: stream over sand.

been a matter for the civil courts only. By attacking the unfortunate Martin, however, the Braes men had committed a crime. In the unwieldy jargon used to describe such occurrences, they had interfered with an officer of the law, a court official in this case, in the execution of his duty. And the authorities were thus enabled to move against them with all the force that could be mustered for that task.

To one man, in particular, this was a most welcome opportunity. His name was William Ivory. He was sheriff of Inverness-shire. And he had precious little time for what he clearly regarded as the nonsensical, if not seditious, notion that the Braes crofters were entitled to be treated with more respect than had been accorded to their counterparts at Boreraig and Suisnish some thirty years before.

Sheriff Ivory, in his own estimation at any rate, stood for rather more than the impartial upholding of the law. Nor was he prepared to confine his sphere of operations to his Inverness courtroom. As events were to prove, he was all too prone to regard himself as nothing less than Queen Victoria's viceroy in the county for which he was responsible. And it was in the manner of just such an imperial legate — as if he were, for all the world, a colonial official dealing with a band of unruly and rebellious tribesmen from the back country — that William Ivory decided to take personal charge of the expeditionary force which he now planned to send against the Braes crofters.

There were not, as it happened, sufficient policemen in Inverness-shire for

Ivory's purpose. Urgent appeals for assistance were duly issued to other Scottish forces. And because the speediest affirmative response was the one which came from Glasgow, it duly transpired that, on the morning of 19 April, 1882, a day of cold, wind-driven rain, a detachment of 50 Glasgow constables took the Braes road from Portree. They were wet. They were chilled. And as they tramped morosely across the bridge that crosses the River Varragill and set off to repeat the journey which had ended so disastrously for Sheriff-Officer Martin a bare twelve days before, they must have wished themselves back in the comparative comfort of Sauchiehall Street and they must have roundly cursed Sheriff William Ivory who, in the style of an officer and a gentleman, was bringing up the rear of the advancing column in a weathertight and well provided carriage.

Past Peinmore they marched and on past Camastianavaig, Conordan, Achnahannait, Upper and Lower Ollach; until, at Gedintailor, they reached Braes proper and could set about discharging their mission: the apprehension of the five men alleged to have taken the most prominent part in the earlier maltreatment of Sheriff-Officer Martin whom Ivory was increasingly inclined to portray as something of a martyr in the cause of keeping the queen's peace.

A watery light was just beginning to be discernible in the sky over Raasay when the police phalanx squelched through Gedintailor. And still there was no sign of trouble. Ivory, in the best tradition of the North-West Frontier, had been determined to mount a dawn assault. And at such a time, and on such a day, the Braes people were less well organised than they might have been. Soon the five wanted men had been arrested. And at once their captors made to return with them to Portree.

Spring muir burning, Borve.

This was not to be easily accomplished, however. While the police had been busy searching half-awakened homesteads down in Peinchorran, the Braes people had begun to gather in some strength at the northern end of Gedintailor; at the place, in fact, where I came to try my hand at stone-throwing a century later. They were in angry mood this crowd. And their objective was as reckless as it was straightforward. They intended to bar the only exit from Braes and to make Ivory and his police contingent relinquish their newly acquired prisoners.

The spot they chose was well adapted for their purpose. Above the road, then little more than a heavily rutted track, is that steep, stony slope I have already mentioned. On the seaward side is a narrow strip of turf and then a sheer drop to the Sound of Raasay; grey, wind-scuffed and cheerless, beyond doubt, on that dull April morning. To force a passage through a sizeable and grimly hostile mob in control of such a position could not have been other than an extremely dangerous and very difficult job.

Even before they had won through to Gedintailor, Ivory's now withdrawing men were involved in a running fight with the Braes folk. Insults were hurled. Sticks were brandished threateningly. A few blows were exchanged. And then, at that readily defended pass, and with the sleety rain still swirling round the combatants, battle was joined in deadly earnest.

From the hillside there came a growing hail of jagged rocks. Blood flowed freely in the rain. People screamed incessantly. Women in home-spun shawls

Broadford Bay.

fought furiously beside their men; fought rather more determinedly in the opinion of some eyewitnesses. The air, reported the newspapermen who had tagged along in Ivory's wake in the hope of some such confrontation, was as thick with Gaelic imprecations as with missiles. And when the police, on Ivory's orders, drew their batons and charged the crowd, both curses and stones flew all the faster. A number of crofters, and at least an equal number of policemen, were more or less badly hurt. Ivory himself fell twice, missing his footing as the opposing throngs surged back and forth on the muddy, confined and slippery piece of ground at the centre of the struggle. But then, just as it seemed that the Braes people were about to achieve their aim of liberating the five captives, a final desperate charge took the police detachment through the encircling mass of yelling, shouting crofters. At a run, and in a state of some disorder, the forces of law and order at once retreated to the comparative safety of Portree.

* * *

Following their route this morning, I climb the roadside fence and turn northwards. A car has stopped and a tourist couple are examining the little stone and concrete monument which stands at the crest of the brae leading out of Gedintailor. The monument is a recent one. For far too long the island's inhabitants have not been encouraged to have any regard for the significance of what happened here. Now these words are helping to put that right:

> faisg air a' charn seo
> air an 9mh latha deug de 'n ghiblein 1882,
> chriochnaich an cath a chuir muinntir a'bhraighe
> air sgath tuath na gaidhealtachd

> near this cairn
> on the 19th of April 1882,
> ended the battle fought by the people of Braes
> on behalf of the crofters of Gaeldom

As that inscription implies, though the day itself went to William Ivory, his triumph was marred by a good deal more than the indignity he had endured. Suitably lurid accounts of proceedings at Braes, wired from the suddenly overwhelmed telegraph office at Portree, were on the nation's breakfast tables the following morning. And the nation, by and large, did not take kindly to the idea of a daybreak descent on people generally portrayed in the press as peaceful villagers tried beyond endurance by their landlord. Public opinion was on the side of the crofters; not on the side of Lord Macdonald. And the crofting community's grievances and aspirations, which had never before attracted much attention outside the Scottish Highlands, were suddenly forced on to the United Kingdom's political and parliamentary agenda.

* * *

The results of this quite novel southern interest in the island's crofting tenants began to be evident on 8 May, 1883, at the small, stone-built church which then served the Braes townships. It is semi-ruinous now, its door barred and its surroundings obviously neglected. But on that spring morning it was at the centre of important happenings. All around were throngs of onlookers; crofters and their families from Peinchorran, Balmeanach, Gedintailor, the two Ollachs, Achnahannait, Conordan, Camastianavaig, Peinmore, Penifiler and further afield; people from Portree; journalists from a score of national and provincial newspapers; officious looking and evidently self-important civil servants from Inverness and Edinburgh. The latter had come down from Portree a little earlier in a succession of carriages, themselves objects of considerable interest in a place where almost everyone went everywhere on foot. And now more such carriages were arriving in a clatter of sweating horses. From these conveyances, the best Skye could provide, there stepped six men who were to have a profound effect on all the subsequent history of the island. Collectively they constituted the royal commission which Mr Gladstone had established a couple of months before 'to inquire into the condition of the crofters and cottars in the Highlands and Islands of Scotland'.

At their head was Francis Napier, Baron of Napier and Ettrick, graduate of Trinity College, Cambridge, a Borders landowner and a career diplomat who had been governor of Madras in India. Then came Donald Cameron of Lochiel, an old Harrovian married to a duke's daughter, lord lieutenant of Inverness-shire as well as the county's Conservative MP. Lochiel, too, was a landowner; as was the commission's third member, Sir Kenneth MacKenzie of Gairloch, a man with no fewer than 170,000 acres to his name. Accompanying Sir Kenneth was Alexander Nicolson, sheriff-substitute at Kirkcudbright and, before that, a successful advocate in Edinburgh. Also from Edinburgh came Donald MacKinnon, Scotland's first professor of Celtic and, as such, a fluent Gaelic speaker. That should, perhaps, have counted in his favour. But the more sceptical of the island's crofters had already noted that, although neither Nicolson nor MacKinnon were landowners in the style of Napier, Lochiel and MacKenzie, the one was a landlord's son and the other was a Tory. Of the six members of the royal commission, in fact, only one was thought to be in any way sympathetic to the crofting cause: Charles Fraser Mackintosh, Liberal MP for Inverness Burghs and a longstanding campaigner for at least a measure of Highland land reform.

Skye crofters, then, expected little from the royal commission. The island's landed gentry, on the other hand, believed that its findings, as one of their representatives had put it, would 'vindicate many sorely maligned proprietors and factors from the charges made against them by untruthful outside agitators'. Both sides were to be proved entirely wrong.

*   *   *

His name, said the first of almost 800 witnesses who were to appear before the commission over the following five months, was Angus Stewart. He was a crofter and fisherman at 5 Peinchorran, Braes. He had been, he confirmed, 'freely elected by the people to be their delegate'.

'Now,' said Lord Napier, these details having been duly recorded, 'will you have the goodness to state to me what are the hardships or grievances of which the people complain who elected you?'

'Yes,' replied Angus Stewart, 'but it is in Gaelic that I prefer to speak.'

To this Napier promptly agreed. And there came forward, from the press of the people in the little church, Portree's sheriff-clerk depute, Dugald McLachlan. As had been previously arranged, he was to serve as the royal commission's interpreter; and, from this point forward, Napier's questions and Stewart's answers would be relayed through him.

'Then you will have the goodness to state,' Napier repeated, 'what are the hardships or grievances of which the people complain who have elected you?'

Back came Stewart's response; to be taken down not only by the commission's shorthand writers but by every reporter in the church. Here, they recognised, was something well worth including in the stories that would appear next day in all the nation's newspapers.

'I would wish that I should have an opportunity of saying a few words before I tell that,' Stewart said carefully, 'and that is that I should have the assurance that I will not be evicted from my holding by the landlord or factor as I have seen done already. I want the assurance that I will not be evicted; for I cannot bear evidence to the distress of my people without bearing evidence to the oppression and high-handedness of the landlord and his factor.'

The crofters mustered on the hard, wooden pews behind Stewart no doubt nodded their assent. His opening statement had been well rehearsed. Every one of them shared his fears. All this Francis Napier took in at a glance. Later he was to write of how impressed he had been by the sincerity and forthrightness of the men who had appeared before him. Today he set out to win their trust; and, in the course of the exchange that followed, the Braes people began to believe that they were, after all, to get a fair hearing from this commission of inquiry.

'It is impossible for the commission to give you any absolute security of the kind which you desire,' said Napier to Stewart. But others, as the commission's chairman well knew, could give that assurance. All eyes turned to Alexander MacDonald, Lord Macdonald's factor. Perhaps he would guarantee that neither Angus Stewart nor his fellow crofters would be placing themselves in jeopardy by giving honest answers to the questions put to them. 'We trust,' Napier added, making clear his own position, 'that no act of oppression or severity would ever be exercised towards you or anyone else by the landlord in consequence of your courage and goodness in telling the absolute truth.'

Alexander MacDonald, however, did not take such a straightforward view of the matter. 'In the first place,' he observed, 'I may say that I am surprised at this man's statement because he is not one of our crofters at all. He is a crofter's son; he is not a crofter.'

This infuriated Angus Stewart. 'I want to say a few words in English,' he interjected angrily. 'It seems that Mr MacDonald objects to my evidence because I am only a crofter's son. My great-grandfather was in Peinchorran. I do not say he was born there; but my grandfather was born in Peinchorran and lived in Peinchorran 86 years. He died there. My mother was born there and is living there yet at the age of 84. I am 40 years of age and I am living in Peinchorran. I am married and have a family. I have been paying rent in Peinchorran to Lord Macdonald for 15 or 16 years and I think I have the right to bear evidence today.'

'You have been elected a delegate by the people of the place,' Lord Napier reassured him, 'and that is quite sufficient for us.'

But, elected delegate or not, Angus Stewart had still to hear from Alexander MacDonald that he would not be removed from his croft for giving voice to the Braes people's quite obvious conviction that they had been maltreated by their laird. Again the commissioners and their audience turned expectantly to Alexander MacDonald.

'I do not think,' the factor commented, 'that he has any reason whatsoever, or that any person has any reason whatsoever, if he tells the truth and nothing but the truth, to fear anything.'

But who was to say what was the truth? And if the decision were to rest with Lord Macdonald and his agents, might they not claim subsequently that statements which reflected badly on them were untrue — and that they were freed, in consequence, from the somewhat grudging undertaking which Alexander MacDonald had just given.

And so Francis Napier again pressed the factor on this point. 'There is something rather ambiguous in the statement which you have made,' he said.

A moment's rest at a fank, North Skye.

'Am I to understand that you publicly state that no proceeding will be taken against any tenant or inhabitant of this place in consequence of what they state before the commission on this occasion?'

'I believe not,' Alexander MacDonald answered. 'You say you believe not,' an increasingly irate Napier returned. 'But do you engage that no proceedings will be taken?'

Conscious, perhaps, that such evasiveness was not exactly helping the landowning lobby's case, Cameron of Lochiel, too, pressed MacDonald for the desired response. It was not forthcoming. Prompted to concede that 'however erroneous or false' he might think a crofter's evidence to the commission, he would not sanction that crofter's eviction, the factor stubbornly refused to commit himself. 'We expect the people will tell the truth,' he responded. 'The people have full liberty to say everything they have to say,' he added.

'But let us come to the point in this matter,' Lord Napier interrupted. 'Will you state yes or no in reply to my question? Will you authorise me to state absolutely to this man that nothing will ever be done prejudicial to his interest, or that of his family, in consequence of anything he may say on this occasion?'

The words yes and no, however, were not in Alexander MacDonald's vocabulary. 'I believe I am quite at liberty to say so,' he replied. And with that Lord Napier and Angus Stewart had to be content. He would now, the latter assented, give his testimony. And devastating testimony it was.

The Braes people, he insisted, were poor; that was the only word to be applied to them. They were poor because they did not have enough land. And they did not have enough land because the island's crofters had been confined to overcrowded and congested corners such as Braes in order that the bulk of the available territory, of which there was certainly no natural scarcity, could be converted into sheep farms and deer forests.

In his grandfather's time, Angus Stewart told the royal commission, there had been five tenants in Peinchorran. Now there were 27. Crofts had been halved, then halved again, on the instructions of successive factors who were themselves under orders to find space for people deprived of their own land because that land was required for other purposes by Lord Macdonald.

'I remember the factor clearing a township,' the Peinchorran crofter went on, 'and devoting the township's land to the purpose of the deer forest.' The township in question, he said, was Torramhichaig on the southern side of Loch Sligachan. It had been cleared in the 1850s. He had been a boy at the time and he recalled how one dispossessed widow and her family had been settled by the factor on his father's holding — 'with the intention,' as he put it, 'that my father would share with her the peats and the half of the croft.' His father had naturally resisted this proposal. However, 'when he went to the factor to complain of this proceeding the factor told him that if he would not give her room he would not have a sod on Lord Macdonald's property.'

His own croft, commented Angus Stewart, for which he paid an annual rent of £5 9s. — the equivalent, then, of more than two months' average wages — was 'rocky, mossy land'. And because that land had been cropped continuously for the past 30 years, since the time, in fact, when increasing congestion had made any kind of crop rotation quite impossible, its fertility, not very great to begin with, had declined to such an extent that the returns from it did not amount to the equivalent of the seed put into it each spring.

'You have stated,' Lord Napier broke in, 'that your great grievances are confined to old land which has been exhausted and which no longer produces a crop. Can you suggest, in general terms, any measure which the landlord or other parties could take in order to improve your situation?'

Angus Stewart had prepared himself for such a question. 'It is easy to answer that,' he declared. 'Give us land, out of the plenty that is about, for cultivation.' There were at least thirty large farms in Skye, he pointed out; 'and there are many of these capable of supporting hundreds of families in comfort'. These farms had maintained substantial populations in the past, he asserted. All that was required was that the land which had been taken away from the people by their lairds should now be restored to them. 'That is the principal remedy I see,' Angus Stewart remarked. 'Give us land at a suitable rent.' There was really no more to be said.

* * *

Leaving the empty church that was the scene of these long ago encounters, I turn back towards Gedintailor. On that May morning in 1883, the birches by the road would have just been coming into leaf; maybe the first cuckoos of the year would have been calling in the little, straggling wood between the church and the sea. Primroses would have been in flower; and the straight, soft, sappy stems of the new bracken would have still been under half a metre tall. Today the season is more advanced. The birch trees are yellowing slightly. Nuts are ripening on the hazel bushes and the rowans are hung with rapidly reddening berries. It is pleasantly warm in the sun: a good day for walking.

I make for Peinchorran, taking the lower of the two roads through Balmeanach, standing aside only very occasionally to allow a car to pass. After four or five kilometres, the road stops abruptly at a spot on the south-eastern flank of Ben Lee, just above the entrance to Loch Sligachan. And from the grassy bank beyond the turning place at the road's end, I watch the Raasay ferry, its wash a spreading white stain on the still water, pull away from the jetty at Sconser. Over there, not far from the ferry terminal, is Sconser Lodge. Once it provided accommodation for the sportsmen — among them, perhaps, the toffs whom Christian Watt observed in Lord Macdonald's company that day in Kyleakin— who came to Skye to take advantage of the first-rate stalking available in the deer forest created by the men responsible for the clearance of Torramhichaig. Now the lodge is one of Skye's many hotels. On its eastern side are the green fields of Torramhichaig itself. They are now part of a golf course.

I have come down here to the road's end with a purpose: to visit 5 Peinchorran, the croft once occupied by Angus Stewart and now the home of Sorley MacLean or, in Gaelic, Somhairle MacGill-Eain.

Sorley MacLean was born in 1911 in Raasay. He went south to university. He taught in schools in Mull and Skye and Edinburgh. He served in the army during the Second World War. He became headmaster of the secondary school at Plockton, over on the mainland not far from Kyle of Lochalsh. He is now retired. And he is, say those who ought to know, the best and the most eminent Gaelic poet of the past century or more.

I have no skill in such matters. My conversations with this deep and deliberate man have been about the past rather than poetry; for in his head he carries knowledge of a kind that was once common on the island but which is now becoming rarer with every year that passes; knowledge based not so much on history books as on an intimate acquaintance with long and intricate skeins of genealogy and family tradition stretching back and forth across the centuries.

Today I want to ask Sorley MacLean about this Angus Stewart; who he was; what happened to him; how he came to be a spokesman, not just for his own township in Peinchorran here, but for crofters everywhere. Remember his opening statement to Francis Napier: 'I cannot bear evidence to the distress of my people without bearing evidence to the oppression and high-handedness of the landlord and his factor.' Ever since I first came across them on the first of the 2000-odd pages of printed testimony to the royal commission of 1883, these proud and defiant words have seemed to me to embody a claim to leadership of a kind to which the likes of the then Lord Macdonald, for all his supposedly chieftainly status, could never have aspired. And so I wish to find out a little more about Angus Stewart.

Sorley MacLean meets me at his gate. 'You see these trees,' he says, indicating the little clump of twisted hawthorns beside us. 'They were planted by Angus Stewart.'

Inside, Sorley places a log or two on the fire and we talk about Braes and about the events of that April morning in 1882. Why did the Braes men not go on to storm the jail in Portree and release Sheriff Ivory's prisoners, Sorley wonders. There was talk of that, he says. But he has heard that the men who planned to march on Portree were met by the minister who persuaded them to desist. Sorley MacLean is not too keen on ministers.

Yes, he agrees, many Braes people did come here after their removal from other places. Braes, he has written somewhere, was the 'dumping ground of the cleared'. And there was no scarcity of people to be dumped. There were so many evictions, you see; thousands of them, yes thousands; in Sleat, in Strath, in Minginish, in Bracadale; on the Macdonald lands, on the MacLeod lands; everywhere. His own family, on his mother's side, were affected by the clearance of Torramhichaig over there. And his Matheson great-grandfather had lost his croft in Staffin because he had built himself a better house. As I will know well enough, such things were not at all unusual. The croft, you see, would have been taken to provide a good home for an estate employee of some kind; an under-factor, a ground-officer; someone like that.

'Angus Stewart,' says Sorley MacLean, 'was my great-granduncle.' And as Stewart told the royal commission, Sorley confirms, he was married and had a family. That family, Sorley goes on, consisted of seven daughters. There were no sons. A number of these daughters emigrated to Canada. Others of them stayed here on Skye.

His wife had died before him and Angus Stewart, then a fairly old man, had gone to stay with his sister. And both brother and sister, as things turned out, died on the same day. Both were among the many island victims of the terrible influenza epidemic which followed the First World War.

Sorley MacLean has in his possession, he says, a copy of a Peinchorran rental dating from 1733. That was long before the township was divided into crofts, of course. But among its three rent-paying tenants at that time were two men by the name of Stewart, Angus and John.

There would have been other people living in Peinchorran then. But the fact that the Stewarts were paying rent directly to Sir Alexander Macdonald of Sleat, instead of to some other intermediate tenant, shows them to have been a family of more than average significance. The Angus Stewart who appeared before Lord Napier was a Peinchorran crofter just like any other. But would his comparatively elevated antecedents have had anything to do with the Peinchorran people's selection of him as their representative?

Sorley MacLean is not sure. Certainly, he says, all the Stewarts had the reputation of being intelligent people. It has been said that the Stewarts brought the 'brains' into his own family. And, whatever the truth of that, they were clearly people of some considerable merit. I will have heard of Norman Stewart from Valtos, Sorley MacLean continues. Indeed I have. He was the man they called 'Parnell' in recognition of the fact that, in the 1880s, he roused the Staffin crofters against their landlord in much the same way as his more

Sorley MacLean.

36

Tower, Uig.

widely renowned Irish counterpart, Charles Stewart Parnell, roused Ireland against the English. Well, explains Sorley, this 'Parnell' was of the same family as Angus Stewart from Peinchorran.

Where these Stewarts came from originally, Sorley MacLean is not completely certain. But it is known that they have been in the island for a long, long time. And it is said that the first of them to settle in Skye was an Appin man. Appin, in the northern part of Argyll, was Stewart country. And the first of the Skye Stewarts is believed to have been a weaver who, in breach of all convention and with the same verve as Angus Stewart displayed in the Braes church that May morning in 1883, married the daughter of a chief — Stewart of Appin, no doubt — and had to run away in consequence. That, at any rate, is the story which Sorley MacLean has heard.

We turn to other topics. Eventually I leave and make my way back to my car. I drive towards Portree along the road once taken by Francis Napier and his colleagues; by Sheriff William Ivory and his tired and frightened policemen; and, much more frequently, by Angus Stewart of Peinchorran. Needing petrol, I stop at a filling station. It belongs, Sorley MacLean told me earlier, to a man descended from Angus Stewart; a man descended ultimately from that weaver who, several hundred years ago in Appin, had the temerity to court and wed his chieftain's daughter.

Alexander MacDonald, Portree solicitor and factor to Lord Macdonald at the time of the troubles in Braes, was called, by his many crofter critics, 'the uncrowned king of Skye'; for, in addition to running the Macdonald properties, he administered the extensive lands belonging to MacLeod of MacLeod, Fraser of Kilmuir, MacDonald of Skeabost and Macalister of Strathaird. Of the 17,000 people living on the island in the 1880s, therefore, only 2000 were beyond Alexander MacDonald's factorial jurisdiction. And even they would almost certainly have come in contact with *Alasdair Ruadh*, as he was also known, in one or other of his virtually innumerable public and private capacities: clerk to the school boards in Portree, Snizort, Stenscholl, Kilmuir, Duirinish, Strath and Bracadale; one of only three bank agents on the island; captain of volunteers, distributor of postage stamps and collector of taxes.

That any individual should have accumulated so much power and influence was obviously undesirable. But I find it difficult not to have some admiration for this sturdy, immensely energetic man whose own small estate at Treaslane, on the western side of Loch Snizort, was thought to be so well managed by its tenants that they were the only Skye crofters to make no complaint to the royal commission of 1883. 'I am very proud of my tenants,' MacDonald remarked on that occasion, 'and very much obliged to them.' He was equally proud of his own success and of the undoubted personal achievement which it represented. 'I am at my work generally from ten in the morning till one next morning and sometimes two,' he said. 'I think I have worked as hard as any working man in the north of Scotland.'

A century on from Alasdair Ruadh, the island seems to have swopped rule by dictator for government by bureaucracy. Skye's population was halved in the last century. During the same period, the number of people in administrative positions in the island has increased by a factor of several hundred. And those parts of Portree which are not given over to hotels and guest houses are occupied, for the most part, by offices belonging to Skye and Lochalsh District Council, Highland Regional Council, the Highlands and Islands Development Board, the Department of Agriculture and Fisheries for Scotland and half a dozen other public or semi-public bodies. Almost nothing can be accomplished in Skye without the consent of one or more of these organisations. And it may be of some consolation to the shade of Alexander MacDonald, who died comparatively young, that none of them are regarded with any more affection than he was himself.

3

PORTREE'S main street is full of people jostling one another off the
pavements. The shops are busy. It is the afternoon of the day of the Skye
Games, one of those supposedly traditional Highland gatherings so roundly
condemned by one nineteenth-century radical who said that such spectacles
depended on working men being persuaded, against their own best interests,
to bare their chests and tear their guts for the pleasure and amusement of a
corrupting and corrupted aristocracy. There is still some risk of muscular
strain from hammer-throwing and caber-tossing, no doubt. But these sports
are increasingly dominated now by a handful of semi-professional athletes
who travel from one such occasion to another. And the audience, too, has
changed. The island gentry, in their bonnets and their kilts, are still in evidence
here and there. But tourists, raising and lowering their umbrellas in the
intermittent drizzle, now constitute the bulk of the spectators.

The games, then, have the slightly contrived air associated with all the
many pageants and spectacles which Britain — like some impoverished
grandee trying to make a desperately needed pound or two by displaying the
relics of her more lavish past — stages for the benefit of fee-paying foreigners.
The resulting artificiality of the various performances on offer means that the
games are incapable of arousing those genuine local passions which are still to
be glimpsed, and more than glimpsed, at a shinty match, for example. But the
games, for all that, continue to draw crowds. And, in this tourist town, crowds
are important.

Portree's information centre, where you can learn what's on in Skye and
ask about the availability of accommodation, is to be found in the town's
former jail where Sheriff William Ivory deposited the crofters whom he
captured in Braes on that eventful April morning in 1882. And today, as it
happens, you may well end by reflecting that the Braes men at least knew
where they were going to spend the night. No, say the women working here,
they're sorry but the Royal Hotel is fully booked; and the Portree Hotel; and
the Coolin Hills; and the Caledonian. A guest house, perhaps? Yes, they think

Tug of War, Skye Games.

they can still offer something there. If you'd just wait a minute while they make a phone call.

So much activity of this kind is unusual now. The tourist industry — its health measured officially by that most infelicitously named invention, the bed night occupancy index — is not what it was in the heady years of the 1960s. Then hundreds of visitors to the island, unable to find a vacant room, spent the hours of darkness dozing uncomfortably in their cars. Then a family might hang out a *bed and breakfast* sign and take in trade with no more difficulty than was involved in catching a mackerel on a summer's evening. But neither mackerel nor tourists are so plentiful today; and though Skye can get by without the former, the comparative scarcity of the latter is a serious business.

The island's economy is heavily dependent on the holidaymakers who come here. That is a fact. And it would be as sensible to maintain that Skye's climate is essentially dry and sunny as to give any other impression. As to the wider implications of this reliance on tourism: well, there you are on altogether more debatable territory.

'Take this bridge,' says the man beside me in a Portree bar. It is a public bar, not a lounge; and, as its spartan furnishings make clear, it is meant to cater primarily for local residents. This, in the circumstances, is probably just as well. 'You know that there's talk of building a bridge to Skye.' Yes, I nod, I've heard. 'Well, I'm all for it,' the man says, 'all for it, you understand. I have to cross that bloody ferry three or four times a week. Hours it wastes, bloody hours. So what do I see in the paper this week? I see that the hotel people here don't want a bridge because once we have a bridge we won't be a proper island and if we aren't a proper island then the tourists might stop coming. So that's the way of it. I've to sit down there in that damn ferry queue, week in week out for the rest of my life, just so that some effing Englishman, who comes here maybe only once if he comes at all, can have the thrill of knowing Skye's a proper bloody island.'

Elsewhere, too, there are strong feelings. 'Do you know what some people here do for the tourists,' one person asks me. 'Come April or May, they walk right out of their houses and go and live for months on end in a shed or a caravan or something. And then they rent out their own homes to crowds of perfect strangers! Can you imagine that sort of thing going on in any other part of the country? Of course you can't. Most people would have more pride. They'd sooner starve than carry on·the way that these poor buggers do!'

People who make that sort of comment, of course, do not normally want to be identified. In Skye, tourism is a sensitive topic. The people who matter in the place are almost invariably on the tourist industry's side. Often they are involved financially in hotels and other holiday enterprises. To be overtly critical of the tourist business, or of its effects on the life of the island, is to put yourself at odds with the establishment, then. And that, especially in a small community, is seldom prudent. 'For me to say out loud that I don't like tourism,' says the man in the bar, 'would be like my grandfather having got on a soapbox out there in Somerled Square and announcing to the world he didn't like landlords. It wouldn't do me any more good than it would have done him, if you see what I mean.'

I see what he means alright. But I also discover that not everyone who welcomes the summer influx does so solely as a consequence of having a vested interest in it. 'When I get into the pulpit in August,' an island minister tells me, 'I feel a little bit better in my mind just because there are strange faces in the congregation; people from other parts of the country, other parts of the world; people I don't meet every day of the year. So I like to see the holidaymakers coming. I think they brighten up the island, make it a wee bit more alive.'

I understand — or I believe I understand — the point the minister is making. 'What tourists bring each year,' the social anthropologist Hugh Brody once wrote about a village in the west of Ireland, 'are numbers, girls, money and reassurance.' And that, to some extent at least, is true of the island also.

It gave people a renewed sense of confidence in their declining and depopulated communities, Brody maintained, to know that outsiders thought these communities worth visiting. And while it was good to have access to some of the cash the tourists spent, he went on, it was even better to be exposed to the more intangible effects of their presence. Because of tourism, and only because of tourism, Brody insisted, pubs that would otherwise have been half empty were suddenly full. There were women in bars that were usually reserved for men. There was more talking, more laughter, more singing, more zest, more enthusiasm.

I do not think that Skye is as far gone in decay as the Irish locality Brody described. But I do believe it is similarly boosted by its annual injection of holidaymakers. For most of the last 150 years, after all, the island's population has been falling. Once there were more than 23,000 people living here. Now there are not much more than a third of that number. And the summer visitors, however temporarily, can and do help to make good the deficiency. Not just churches, but also shops and pubs, are busier, brighter and more invigorating. Hotels and restaurants, all too often closed in winter, are open and well patronised. There are many more children and teenagers to be seen. There is opened up, if only for a moment, a window into the thickly peopled world that was lost when Suisnish, Boreraig and so many other communities were destroyed.

Competitor practising at the Skye Games.

And then there is the money tourism brings, its advocates tell you. Look at what's spent here in the summer. Millions, yes, millions. How many families could keep going without what they make by doing *bed and breakfast*? How many garages and shops would have to close if it wasn't for the extra custom they get every summer? Oh, yes, people complain about the tourists. They can't get past their caravans on the road, they say. They have to stand and wait their turn in the post-office, they say. People are too busy to stop and speak to you, they say. But without tourism, I'm telling you, this place would be dead, finished. And that's the truth. They'd be as well to take away the ferry and evacuate the whole island.

I agree, of course; there is, in a sense, no scope for disagreement. The figures support the man's case. And so do the organisations which produce the figures: the regional council, the district council, the Highlands and Islands Development Board and all the rest. Take the Highland Board, for instance. For most of the last twenty years it has spent as much, or even more, on tourism as on agriculture, fisheries and manufacturing combined. That has not been done frivolously. The men who direct the board's operations, from its Inverness headquarters, are obviously convinced that such investment brings the best returns in terms of providing employment in places like Skye; and the men who run the board presumably know exactly what they are about. Or do they?

Not everybody in Skye thinks so. Hoteliers are naturally on the side of the Highland Board. Hotel workers are often less enthusiastic and grumble about long hours, low pay and a total lack of job security. There are island hotels, it must be stressed, which take on the same staff summer after summer, and pay them comparatively well. But because the industry is essentially seasonal, with many hotels closing completely for the winter months, there is said to be a tendency on the part of some owners and managers to cut costs by keeping staff wages low and by filling staff posts with relays of students and other temporary workers from the south — or even from overseas. And when that happens, of course, the hotel in question ceases to provide the surrounding community with additional income of any kind.

'Well, yes,' my pro-tourism acquaintance remarks when I put this point to him. 'There's something in that right enough. But there's more to this business than hotels, you know. Take the *bed and breakfast* places now. There the money's coming straight into local homes; out of the tourist's pocket and into the Skye housewife's purse, so to speak. You go and talk to some of the *bed and breakfast* landladies and see what they've to say.'

But nothing to do with tourism on the island is ever quite so simple as it seems. Yes, affirm the women to whom I talk, they do rely a fair bit on 'doing B and B'. Yes, the returns from it are not too bad as long, that is, as you discount your own time and labour. Yes, it can be enjoyable. You meet different people. Often they're nice, friendly, interesting, appreciative.

But no, it's not without its snags. Well, nothing ever is. You get tired of guests who come in late at night and expect you to be on hand, all smiling and hospitable, to give them cups of tea and answer all their questions. They forget you have to be up at six the next morning to get your man out to his work, to get the kids ready for school, to make them their breakfast.

'But the worst thing,' one woman tells me, 'is the total lack of privacy. For months, you see, your home isn't what you could call your own. There are strangers in it all the time. You live in the kitchen while they live in the sitting room. They get the best of treatment. Your own family are left to get by as best they can. So, yes, it's a strain. Well, I mean, there's the fact that there are always other people overhearing you. You don't like to sing. You can't swear. You can't shout. You even have to fight in whispers.

'You know how some of the old people, in particular, put a sack over the *bed and breakfast* notice on a Sunday. That's supposed to be because of it being the sabbath and the church insisting that, on the sabbath, you do nothing in the way of work. People from other places laugh at such a notion, I suppose. Some of them even get quite cross about it. What's the point of us inviting tourists here, they say, if we're going to turf them out on Sundays. Well, I don't know. The religious side of it is neither here nor there as far as I'm concerned. But I think people are entitled to one day out of seven when they can just be by themselves.'

* * *

If you are simply a tourist, of course, it is sufficient to take Skye as you find it. And, if you are fortunate, you will find it beautiful. On a summer's evening, driving out of Kyleakin, I stop to give a lift to a couple of hitchhikers. They are German, I discover. They come from Dusseldorf. And to them the island seems a place of wonder. Look, they exclaim, as we approach Breakish and the clouds begin to break after the rain. Look at the sky. And they gaze, almost in awe, it seems to me, as the sun, from behind the shoulder of Beinn na Caillich, suddenly illuminates a shining strip of sea and land and mist. They have never before, they say, seen anything like this. To live here must surely be quite perfect.

* * *

That is not the universal opinion. In a muddy field behind one of Skye's many churches I knock on the door of the caravan occupied by two young people to whom the island appears to have very little to offer. They were married two years ago, they explain. But in all that time they have been unable to obtain a house. In all that time this metal box, as one of them calls it, is the only place they have ever been able to call home.

Theirs is not an uncommon experience; for Skye, where so many families were made homeless in the past, has more than its share of homelessness still. And that, in part at least, is a consequence of the fact that the island seems so attractive to its visitors.

Many people who come here do not wish to return only for an occasional week or fortnight in a Skye hotel. Instead they want to acquire their own, more permanent, stake in the island. And so they buy a Skye property; as a holiday home; as a place to which they will one day retire; even, in slightly more unusual cases, as the means to a whole new way of living. But whether these people wish to spend their holidays or their old age here, or whether they have become convinced that they would rather be lobster fishermen than commuters, the effect on the local housing market is the same: prices are pushed beyond the reach of the resident community.

'We're both working,' I am told in that cramped caravan. 'We have reasonable enough jobs by Skye standards. But out of what we're earning we'd never save enough to buy a house if we lived to be a hundred. The holiday home people have seen to that.'

Could they not, then, apply for a council house? Well, yes, they have done that. Their names are on the waiting list. Their names, in fact, have been on the list since they were married. And the way things are going, they say, their names will probably remain there a lot longer.

Skye and Lochalsh District Council is one of Scotland's smallest and least affluent local authorities. Its housing requirements, on a per head of population basis, are as pressing as any in Britain. But the council's financial resources are slim. Its capacity to build the necessary houses is limited. And a number of the houses which it has already constructed — and which have been sold, at government insistence, to their occupants — may well themselves become the holiday homes of the future. The island's housing problems, in other words, are beyond the council's solving.

Outside it has begun to rain again and the water drums on the caravan's roof. 'I go and see the housing officials in Portree every so often. But all I get from them is more excuses. There are always people with much better claims than us; people with nowhere at all; people with children. And so folk have started dropping hints about it being time for us to have a baby. Then we'd be moved up the list, you see, and that might entitle us to something. But it's a hellish way of living, isn't it, when we're supposed to sit down and discuss having a child, not for its own sake, not because we want a son or a daughter, but because that child might be our only way of getting out of here.'

The holiday home owners to whom I speak do not accept any responsibility for the fact that so many of the island's young men and women have to start their lives together in conditions that vary from unsatisfactory to appalling; in mobile houses and caravans of one kind or another; in houses rented to them for the winter only; in a room or two in someone else's house. That has nothing to do with them, the holiday home people say. The places they have bought were previously derelict, dilapidated, ruinous. Nobody was interested in them. Why should they be made to feel guilty about having renovated and restored these tumbledown old cottages?

Objectively, they may be right. Objectively, I suppose, it would not have helped that caravan couple if the ruins that are now nice holiday residences had remained ruins. But when you are one of a social problem's victims, you are not inclined to set much store by an objective assessment of its origins. The woman with whom I'm talking in this caravan this afternoon knows only that

Dawn, Portree Bay.

she has got no home and that other people have got two.

'Come over here to the window,' she says. I squeeze past the folding table that occupies almost all the available floor space and look out across the field where shallow puddles are already forming. 'Do you see that house there,' she asks, 'and that one two along and that one down beside the main road? They're all holiday homes. There's not a light in them all winter. Well, when I'm here alone in the evening then, and its dark and damp and cold, I think a lot about these houses. I think about them belonging to people down in England — people who already have a perfectly good home down there. I think about me not being able to get a house of my own in the island where I was born and in the place where both of us are living and working all year round. And sometimes, you know, I wish that someone here had the guts to do what they did to the holiday homes in Wales and set fire to every one of them.'

The people who maintain holiday homes in Skye come here only occasionally. Those who move permanently to the island, however, are not necessarily more popular. Too many of these incomers are in the habit of attempting to dictate to islanders how local matters should be organised. And so patronising, so superior and so offensive are some of those mostly middle-class and mostly English immigrants that Skye people — feeling themselves, no doubt, to have been cast in the lowly role once reserved for Kenya's and Rhodesia's blacks — have bestowed on the more disliked of these immigrants a designation borrowed from our former African colonies. 'White settlers', they call the new arrivals. And the general attitude towards them is exemplified by a remark made by an exasperated crofter in the course of a public meeting at which a typically vociferous white settler was protesting about the local habit of killing foxes in order to protect lambs. If the incomer in question did not like the way things were done in Skye, said the crofter, then he was quite at liberty to leave. 'And I'll be very pleased,' the crofter added, 'to direct you to the ferry.'

4

THERE are other ways to Skye besides the ferry from Kyle of Lochalsh. There is, for instance, the train to Mallaig and the boat to Armadale. In winter that train would be almost empty. But it is July and every seat is taken, if not by a passenger then by a passenger's luggage in the shape of an overfilled and overbalancing rucksack. In the Highlands and Islands only the relatively poor travel by public transport which is invariably slow and usually unreliable. And the relatively poor consist overwhelmingly, at this time of year, of the younger sort of tourist. The train is full of people in their late teens and early twenties. And when our tickets are inspected, I am shown to be the only person in view who has paid the standard fare. Everyone else hands over discount-priced student tickets of the type that entitle their holders to be shuttled up, down and across the country's rail network for several days, or even a couple of weeks, at a time.

Nowhere on that network is there another route like this one. The train, admittedly, is not the sort that British Rail feature in their advertisements. Its carriages, as always on Highland lines, are old; for from these northern extremities rolling stock goes only to the breaker's yard. The varnish has long since peeled away from the wooden windowframe beside me. My seat both looks and smells well used. And there is a constant creaking and clattering as if the combination of uneven track and ancient carriage might eventually result in bodywork and chassis parting company at some especially tight bend.

'For years the politicians didn't give a shit about the railroad,' a Canadian once complained to me on a train marooned inexplicably in a New Brunswick forest. 'And then along comes the energy crisis and they're all surprised that the goddam railroad isn't working any more.'

The railway to Mallaig is not always working properly either. A bumpy permanent way; a rash of speed limits; a reliance on locomotives which are frequently proved to be unreliable; a tendency to stop where no stop was intended: these are the universal symptoms of a railway's final illness. And the Mallaig line suffers from them all. I have no great confidence, as a result, in its having very much of a future.

That is a pity; for, as I mentioned earlier, it is unique. On this day of brilliant sun and sudden, shattering showers, it steadily unrolls its views of hills and lochs and sea and islands in a more than normally spectacular fashion; sometimes shrouding a mountain in sheeting rain, then exposing the same mountain to a burst of light which reflects dazzlingly from rocks and waterfalls.

The girl with whom I am sharing my seat is called Simone, I discover. She is French. She teaches in Paris. She has not been to Scotland before. She has spent three days in Edinburgh. Now she is on her way to Skye.

We are passing the head of Loch Shiel and the stubby stone tower which marks the spot where the Jacobite standard was raised in 1745 and where there then gathered the small band of soldiers, adventurers, misfits, idealists and incompetents who believed it possible to overthrow an empire and to place on its throne the long exiled representative of a discredited and reactionary royal family who had twice before been removed from that same throne by revolution and rebellion.

Simone has not heard of Bonnie Prince Charlie. Why should she have done? Neither he nor the campaign on which he embarked at this spot that long ago August were of any international significance. Simone's country and its government had landed the prince in Scotland because France was then at war with England and because trouble in England's backyard, so to speak, might make things temporarily easier for France's armies in the places where the war would be won or lost. These places did not include the Scottish Highlands and Islands. Their inhabitants, like Prince Charles Edward Stuart himself, were thought expendable. And so they were duly expended.

Simone asks about the Loch Shiel monument. And as the train trundles towards Lochailort, I tell her a little about the prince and about the armed uprising which he initiated; how it was ill conceived, underfinanced and poorly executed; how it ended, inevitably, in defeat; how it is still at the centre of a silly and belittling romanticism which misrepresents both its participants and its consequences.

'You do not like this Prince Charles,' says Simone. No, I agree, I do not like him; well, not him exactly; more his role in unleashing the avalanche of enforced change which, in the aftermath of his expedition's failure, was to transform both the island and the rest of north-west Scotland and which, in so doing, was to destroy so much that seems to me to have been meritorious.

* * *

It is in this sense that so much of what has happened to the island in the course of the last two centuries might be said to have begun in the late evening of 5 December, 1745, at a place called Swarkstone Bridge in the English Midlands. There, some ten kilometres south of Derby, not much more than 150 kilometres from London, a small group of Gaelic-speaking soldiers, their heavy plaids pulled tightly around their shoulders, huddled together in an

Cloud, Aird Bhearnasdail.

The mouth of the Kilmartin River, Staffin.

attempt to fend off the encroaching chill of the winter's night. These men, all of them carrying muskets and broadswords, were the Jacobite army's advance guard. And they were awaiting orders.

The precise nature of these orders was the subject of furious debate at what passed for the army's headquarter. Prince Charles Edward Stuart — only nominally in charge of affairs and already, perhaps, beginning to seek some consolation in the drink that would later be his means of evading such responsibilities as were to remain to him — was for marching at once on the nation's capital. But his military commanders refused to sanction such a course. And soon the men at Swarkstone Bridge had been instructed to turn around and to commence the long northward march which ended so bloodily and so disastrously amid the driving sleet and scything grapeshot on Culloden Moor.

So totally have the bare bones of these events been lost to sight beneath the layered lyricism of successive generations of romancers, and so inevitable does Jacobitism's ultimate defeat seem to us who are inescapably aware of the tragedy which was to follow Charles Edward Stuart's escapade, that the sheer military prowess of what had been accomplished is often overlooked. And yet, in rather less than four months, since leaving Glenfinnan at the northern end of Loch Shiel on 19 August, this small, unprofessional and predominantly Highland army of under 5000 men had conquered all of Scotland and gone on to threaten London, the city at the centre of one of the eighteenth-century world's most powerful countries. It was a remarkable achievement. But in its very success is to be found the explanation for the calamity that ensued.

Until 1745, Britain's rulers had been prone to think of places like the island, if they thought of them at all, as faraway localities populated by primitive hill tribes of no very great account. All that was changed by the spectacle of those 5000 Highlanders advancing — as it seemed, at first, inexorably — on London. The prime minister and the cabinet, like the capital's ordinary citizens, were understandably terrified. And in their terror they decided not only that this invading army should be crushed militarily but also that the necessary steps, however drastic, should afterwards be taken to ensure that no such incursion should ever again trouble either the British state or the Hanoverian monarchs at its head.

Hence the sheer ferocity displayed by British troops in Gaelic Scotland in the months following the collapse of Charles Edward Stuart's attempt to take the British crown by force. The reprisals began on Culloden Moor itself where General Henry Hawley ordered his redcoated troops to bayonet every wounded Highlander they found. And as the summer of 1746 advanced, the burnings, killings and executions spread right across the Highlands.

Because Highlanders, like the Irish or, for that matter, the native peoples of America, Africa and Asia, were thought to be an inferior and semi-barbarous race, there was no attempt to apply to the occupying army the comparatively stringent code of discipline which governed the military's dealings with the French, the Spanish and other civilised opponents. Instead the Duke of Cumberland, brother of the king and commander of the government forces in

Tulm Island seen from the fortifications of Duntulm Castle.

Scotland, was given authority, as a despatch to him stated, 'to do whatever is necessary for the suppressing of this unnatural rebellion'. And what was considered necessary did not exclude murder, rape, looting, arson and wanton destruction of every kind.

This carefully calculated and deliberate savagery, however, was merely the prelude to a more insidious onslaught. The traditional social structure of the Highlands and Islands, it emerged, was to be undermined and subverted; and all that was distinctive in the Highland way of life was to be eliminated. The right to carry arms was withdrawn. Highland dress was outlawed. The wearing of tartan was proscribed. Everything possible was done to discourage the use of Gaelic. And, most critically of all, there was developed a triumphantly successful means of separating and dividing ordinary Highlanders from the men who had long been their leaders and commanders.

At the centre of the essentially tribal society which had prevailed for hundreds of years in Skye and other parts of the Highlands were clan chieftains; men like Macdonald of Sleat or MacLeod of Dunvegan; men who traced their ancestry to infinitely remote and sometimes semi-mythical warriors in whose ceaselessly celebrated exploits there can be discerned a fusing of two races which first clashed in the island more than eleven centuries ago, the Gaels and the Vikings.

A clan chief was an aristocrat certainly; no person was ever more conscious than he of his elevated status and his privileged position. But he was also an integral member of the community he headed. He spoke that community's language. He patronised its poets and pipers, its harpists and historians. He embodied its outlook and aspirations. And the island's bards, even in the eighteenth century — the century that witnessed the invention of both the steam engine and the factory, the century of imperial expansion, the American Revolution and the Declaration of the Rights of Man — were all too prone to assume that such would always be the case.

External circumstances, however, had altered far too radically to permit such continuity. Even before Prince Charles Edward Stuart inadvertently brought the roof crashing in on the old order, MacLeod of Dunvegan, Macdonald of Sleat and their like had been increasingly attracted by the more commercial, and less patriarchal, type of society then developing in the south. Now, with the British government out to wean all such former headmen to its side, Highland chieftains were given every encouragement, every incentive, to break completely with their people and to adopt the ethics and ambitions of London's men of power. Their children began to be educated in southern schools. They married into the English aristocracy. They stopped speaking Gaelic. They built fine houses from which their clansfolk, with the exception of those who became their hired servants, were rigorously excluded. They became, in short, the anglicised landlords that their descendants have ever since remained. And in that capacity, as the unchallenged owners of almost all the island, nineteenth-century Macdonald and MacLeod chieftains would subject Skye people, including many thousands of those who shared their names, to a tyranny every bit as merciless as any imposed by Cumberland's dragoons.

* * *

From the train window we watch a small boy drag a bundle of mailbags along a puddled platform. At the door of a nearby croft house, an old man, having painstakingly stoked his lidded pipe, is striking a match on the stone wall beside him. Simone, it transpires, comes originally from the Massif Central where her brother has just taken over the family smallholding. How does the British government's approach to crofting compare with the financial and other assistance available to similar sorts of agriculture in France, she wonders. Not well, we decide.

The train is approaching Mallaig and there is a general retrieving of rucksacks and bedrolls. Simone has discovered that I intend to write about Skye. 'You will not write too much about Bonnie Prince Charlie,' she says. 'You will, I think, write a little more about crofters.'

From the station I walk down to the pier. The boat is waiting. The moist air is heavy with the salt scent of the sea. Across the Sound of Sleat the houses on the island gleam whitely in the sun. Yes, I will not write too much about Bonnie Prince Charlie. And yes, I will write a little bit more about crofters.

* * *

The railway came to both Mallaig and Kyle of Lochalsh in the years around 1900; its advance from its previous terminals at Strome Ferry and Fort William financed largely from public funds. In thus developing what today's economists and planners would call the island's communications infrastructure, the governments of that time were attempting to make crofting unrest of the Braes type less likely by making crofters wealthier. And, in the 1890s, in furtherance of this objective, plans were made for railway construction on Skye itself. A narrow gauge track, it was proposed, should be laid from Kyleakin to Broadford, Sligachan, Portree and Uig with possible branches to Isle Ornsay and Dunvegan.

That particular railway, modelled on similar lines then being laid in the west of Ireland, was never built. And even the limited extension from Strome to Kyle proved much more difficult, and much more expensive, than had been anticipated. Cutting after cutting had to be blasted out of solid rock — as had the site for the new railway's terminus. And though three trains still leave that terminus for Inverness each weekday, Kyle's station has the rather shabby look of an enterprise operated by men lacking any real faith in its viability. From Kyle to Inverness by rail takes two hours and forty minutes. By road, the journey can be accomplished in not much more than an hour and a half. And it is by road, down through Glen Shiel and on to Kyle by way of Dornie and Balmacara, that most people now come to Skye.

But the nineteenth-century railwaymen who first made Kyle the island's foremost point of contact with the mainland also ensured that the place should forever bear their imprint. Kyle's rocky foreshore is almost entirely occupied by their station, their piers, their jetties and their large, rectangular hotel. The rest of the village, denied any access to the seafront and hemmed in on every side by hills and cliffs, huddles untidily around the busy roads leading to the Skye ferry. Kyle of Lochalsh is not beautiful. But it does not need to be. Its shops and pubs and eating places will be guaranteed a clientele as long as there is interest in getting to the island.

Crossing the Minch from Uist to Uig in Skye on the 'Hebrides'.

Today, then, there are three places on the mainland from which there are ferries to the island. The crossing from Kyle of Lochalsh to Kyleakin is by far the busiest; that from Mallaig to Armadale is the longest. The third, at Kyle Rhea, is the oldest and, though boats operate there now only in the summer months, it seems to me to be still the most enticing.

At Kyle Rhea the tides swirl and churn through the narrows which connect the Sound of Sleat to Loch Alsh and Loch Duich. The swiftness of the water, long a hazard to shipping, seems somehow accentuated by the steepness of the hills on either side. And you approach and leave the ferry slipways by wildly erratic mountain roads which convey an impression — proved totally false, for better or worse, on getting ten kilometres into Skye and coming across Broadford's hotels, pubs and stores — of having penetrated to a still remote and inaccessible locality.

When British army engineers first set out to tame this then wild quarter a couple of centuries ago, they began by pushing a road up and over Bealach Ratagain, 339 metres high at its summit, and on down Glen More to Glenelg and Kyle Rhea. The military barracks dating from that period can still be seen at Bernera at the bottom of Glen More. And the Kyle Rhea ferry still follows the route which would have been familiar to the barrack's occupants; a route which was of more significance in their day than in ours.

Had you come here on any August or September day in the earlier part of last century and sat down on the slopes of Cnoc a' Chomh-ruith, the hillock on the mainland side of the crossing a kilometre or so to the south of the spot where a set of high tension cables have now been slung across the strait, you could have watched the bustle and activity surrounding the sending to market of the black cattle which, before the clearances, were the source of a substantial proportion of such income as was then available to islanders.

The roaring, restless beasts that congregated here at Kyle Rhea were bound for Falkirk. There, in the years around and after 1800, as many as 50,000 cattle were sold each autumn. And of these 50,000, perhaps two-fifths would have been driven overland from the Hebrides.

The Falkirk trysts, as the Stirlingshire town's cattle sales were known, were confused but magnificent affairs where drovers from Skye and the West Highlands — 'dressed usually', noted one contemporary observer, 'in homespun tweeds which smelt of heather and which were so thick that those who wore them looked like bears as they lounged heavily along' — met and mingled and smoked and drank and talked with their counterparts from Caithness, Banffshire and Aberdeenshire.

The selling of their cattle at Falkirk was the undoubted highlight of these men's hard, rough lives. There, in a score of different dialects of Scots and Gaelic and English, drovers from beyond the mountains haggled fiercely and interminably with prospective buyers from the Borders, Cumberland, Yorkshire, Lincolnshire and East Anglia; the southerners strolling from lot to lot, casting an ostentatiously sceptical eye over lean and wiry beasts that had been several weeks on the hoof, talking down each batch's merits as persistently and energetically as the northern drovers did the opposite.

Tarskavaig, Sleat.

Eventually, however, a dealer from the Midlands, say, would make an agreement with a drover from the island. All argument over, the resulting bargain would be settled over a glass of whisky; with the drover, perhaps, being engaged, at the standard rate of a shilling a day, to take the Englishman's newly acquired cattle south through the Cheviots and the Pennines to other great fairs in places like Norfolk and Hertfordshire.

Such epic treks, the equivalent of later and more celebrated droves across the North American prairies and the Australian outback, might last for two or three months. And in all that time, between leaving Skye and arriving at his final destination several hundred kilometres away in England, the drover would have spent not so much as a single night indoors; sleeping always in the open among his jealously guarded cattle; protected from the rain and frost only by the stout tweed plaid in which he wrapped himself before stretching out upon the ground.

Such a man would naturally want to relax a little after his already protracted stint on the hill tracks which linked Falkirk with the island. And at the annual trysts he was not denied that opportunity. The sale ground might stink of cattle, dung, damp cloth, dogs and sweat. But it boasted enormous bonfires on which there simmered equally enormous cauldrons of eagerly consumed, throat-scalding broth, washed down, no doubt, by still more whisky. Alongside the busy tents dispensing drams and ale were banking booths in which a man might deposit his cash. There were also swarms of pickpockets anxious to relieve him of the chance to do so; and there were beggars, quacks, cardsharpers, peddlers, hawkers, professional gamblers and prostitutes all soliciting his attention and all claiming their share of his largesse.

The thousands of animals reaching the Skye side of the Kyle Rhea crossing began their journey, in many instances, in Lewis, Harris and the Uists. There they were driven to Tarbert, Lochmaddy and other harbours where they were loaded on to and into boats of every conceivable description, each vessel's holds and decks being carpeted with springy birch and willow branches to protect its timbers from the impact of the restless cattle's hooves.

The Minch safely crossed, these Outer Isles herds were disembarked at Loch Dunvegan, in the island's north-western corner, by being hoisted unceremoniously over the side of a hove-to ship and left to swim ashore. Back on land, their numbers now swollen by animals from Glendale and Waternish in Skye itself, they were driven on, in easy stages, by way of Bracadale and Glen Drynoch to Sligachan and Sconser. There they might encounter other droves coming down through Braes from Kilmuir, Staffin and Portree. And so, day after day, herd after herd passed through this central portion of the island; rounding Loch Ainort and continuing through Broadford, Harrapool, Skulamus and Breakish to Glen Arroch and Kyle Rhea.

Here, at slack tide when the usually rapid current was temporarily stilled, the noisily nervous cattle were walked in long lines into the sea. 'For this purpose,' wrote one early nineteenth-century witness of the scene, 'the drovers purchase ropes which are cut at the length of three feet, having a noose at one end. The noose is put round the under jaw of every cow, taking care to leave the tongue free.' That particular detail, it seems, was important. Each beast's tongue had to be left unimpeded, it was explained, in order that 'the animal may be able to keep the salt water from going down its throat'. And that there was a very real risk of such drownings can be deduced from even this matter-of-fact account of the operation's next, and trickiest, phase: 'Whenever the noose is put under the jaw, all the beasts are led by the ferryman into the water until they are afloat, which puts an end to their resistance. Then every cow is tied to the tail of the cow before until a string of six or eight be joined. A man in the stern of the boat holds the rope of the foremost cow. The rowers then ply their oars immediately.' And though there was still plenty of scope for error, accidents were surprisingly infrequent. 'The ferrymen are so dexterous,' concluded our watcher from the shore, 'that very few beasts are lost.'

*   *   *

From high on Cnoc a' Chomh-ruith, on this damp and midge-infested summer afternoon, there is no bellowing of harried cattle to be heard; no barking of dogs; no splashing of oars; no shouting and swearing and whistling of drovers: only the steady rumble of the modern ferry's diesel engines and the sporadic chatter of its over-amplified radio telephone. Last century's clearances killed off the droving trade and put the drovers out of business. Today Skye is less an exporter of cattle, more an importer of tourists. And comparatively few of them come this way to the island.

*   *   *

James Boswell and Dr Samuel Johnson took the Glen More and Glenelg

Fishing boat, Portree Bay.

route to Skye in 1773. Johnson, then one of London's leading literary figures, was 63. And most tourists of his age do not now venture far from their cars and coaches. But there were few roads in the Highlands in the eighteenth century and, at the back end of the year when the weather was already turning wild and wintry, Johnson made his journey to the Hebrides on horseback, on foot and in open boats. It was, by any reckoning, a considerable achievement; a testimony to the curmudgeonly old writer's physical stamina as well as to his insatiable inquisitiveness about the world around him.

He had travelled to the island, Johnson admitted, in the hope of discovering here 'a people of peculiar appearance and a system of antiquated life'. He found that he had come too late. 'There was perhaps never any change of national manners so quick, so great and so general as that which has operated in the Highlands by the late conquest and the present laws,' he wrote. Less than twenty years after Culloden, it appeared, the old society had gone, if not beyond recall then certainly beyond recovery. 'The clans retain little now of their original character,' Johnson concluded. 'Their ferocity of temper is softened, their military ardour is extinguished and their reverence for their chiefs abated.' Nor was this other than unavoidable, Johnson thought, in view of the way that the island's aristocrats were so rapidly and so enthusiastically exchanging the role of tribal leader for that of southern-style proprietor. Skye's lairds, Johnson observed, were concerned more and more with nothing save the 'improvement of their revenues'. In consequence, he continued, they had already lost much of the popular respect and affection they had once enjoyed; 'and as they gradually degenerate from patriarchal rulers to rapacious landlords, they will divest themselves of the little that remains'.

Samuel Johnson, an old-fashioned Tory who believed that there should be more to social relations than the unchecked exploitation of one set of people by another, did not view that prospect with much pleasure. Certainly there had been armed rebellion in the Highlands, he conceded. And to the extent that there would be no more such outbreaks, government policy in the region might be said to have succeeded. 'But it affords a legislator little self-applause,' Johnson added, 'to consider that, where there was formerly an insurrection, there is now a wilderness.'

The wilderness is now a good deal more extensive than was the case in Samuel Johnson's time. But the causes of its having become so are those which he identified 200 years ago. He was the most percipient of all the many people to have written about the island. And if I do not refer to him as often as most of his other successors, it is not from any lack of respect; it is merely out of a desire to be a little different.

5

ON leaving Glenelg, Johnson and Boswell made for Sleat, the southern part of Skye. This was Macdonald territory and they were entertained by the Macdonald laird of the day. 'Dr Johnson had been very pleased with him in London,' Boswell observed of the latter gentleman whom he described as an Eton scholar and a man of talent. In Skye, however, Macdonald's evident intention of financing his social ambitions by extracting more and more cash from the people living on his estate seems to have annoyed his visitors almost as much as it angered his tenants. 'My fellow traveller and I were now full of the old Highland spirit,' Boswell wrote, 'and were dissatisfied at hearing of racked rents and emigration.' But for all their dissatisfaction, much more was to be heard of both these topics; for it was here in Sleat that Skye people were first subjected to the full rigours of the new commercial order so disliked by James Boswell and Samuel Johnson.

For centuries the land in Sleat had been parcelled out in ways designed to provide successive Macdonald chieftains with the fighting men they required to maintain their power, prestige and influence. From their chief, each of the clan's more prominent members received a tack or farm. On any such tack there were to be found, in turn, its holder's own retainers; people who jointly occupied such pieces of ground as the tacksmen, or superior tenant, made available to them. And around these lesser tenants there clustered, finally, various grades of cottagers who might, or might not, have a plot which they could call their own.

Such an arrangement owed nothing to economic considerations. It reflected instead the military necessities of the tribal society which inspired it. At times of crisis in the clan's affairs, the chief ordered out his tacksmen; each tacksman ordered out his tenants; each set of tenants ordered out their entire community. And in the battles which invariably followed any such mobilisation, all these individuals and groups performed their own distinctive tasks: the chief provided the necessary generalship; the tacksmen were his officer corps; the tacksmen's tenants were, in effect, the regiment's NCOs;

and those who remained were the private soldiers or enlisted men who, throwing away their plaids and brandishing their broadswords, would make the devastating charges that were the basis of all Highland warfare.

In the changed circumstances of the decades following the Battle of Culloden, however, armed force of the traditional type could no longer be deployed by Highland chieftains. Their place in the world depended now, not on the number of troops they could command, but on the quantities of cash at their disposal. And so Skye's chiefs, as Samuel Johnson noted, 'necessarily turned their thoughts to the improvement of their revenues'. Land which had previously been made available to tacksmen and others in return for military service, rather than money, was now let for a high rent. And soon the ceaseless quest for increased income would take precedence over all the chieftain's traditional responsibilities to a population which he had once led but which he was, increasingly, to exploit, oppress and terrorise.

When Johnson came this way in the 1770s, the new rents were being paid from the prices fetched by black cattle of the type then driven annually to Falkirk. By the eighteenth century's end, however, two novel, and much more lucrative, commodities had put in an appearance. And the brutal readjustments which the island's lairds initiated in order to profit fully from them are still affecting Skye. One of these commodities was wool. The other was kelp, the name given to a crude but effective industrial alkali produced by incinerating a leathery, brown, thick-stemmed seaweed which is common on the island's rocky shores.

Gesto farm with the Cuillin beyond.

The Quirang, Trotternish.

The kelp industry was labour intensive; it required a large workforce. And that workforce, as things turned out, was conveniently to hand in the form of the many families whom Skye's landowners were evicting from those parts of the island best suited to sheep farming. Making kelp, mind you, was a nasty, dismal and unpleasant job. The growing seaweed had to be cut by men and women wading chest deep in icy seawater. It had to be dragged ashore, dried and burned in specially constructed kilns. And though a laird like Lord Macdonald might make as much as £20 from each ton of kelp thus produced, the people who actually provided him with the raw material had to be content with as little as a tenth of that amount.

As long as it was possible for ordinary islanders to make a living by any others means, then, there would be no rush to volunteer for employment in the kelp trade. Recognising this, Skye's landlords, with Lord Macdonald in the lead, resorted to a characteristically unsubtle form of coercion.

Having removed the longstanding occupiers of the best agricultural land, and having handed that land over to incoming sheep farmers who were prepared to pay much higher rents for it, Lord Macdonald settled the families whom he had thus dispossessed on new smallholdings created for that purpose. These holdings were in coastal areas where their tenants would be near the kelp grounds. And unlike traditional island settlements, where the arable as well as the pasture land had always been held in common, these new townships consisted of large numbers of quite separate plots, each of them occupied by a single family. These plots were called crofts. The people who lived on them were called crofters.

The artificiality of these crofting townships was evident in the way they were laid out. A footrule was placed on a large-scale estate map and the boundaries of the different holdings were designated by long, straight, parallel lines. The typical croft, then, was a narrow strip of territory, frequently not much more than a hundred metres wide, running inland from the sea in a manner that is still to be seen all over Skye. The typical croft was also small. Its tenant, if fortunate, might still have access to hill grazings which continued to be held in common. But the better grazings of course, had been allocated to sheep farmers. And the crofter, in consequence, was left with a small share in an inferior piece of hill pasture — together with his own patch of supposedly arable ground, usually no more than a couple of hectares in extent and consisting very often of previously uncultivated bog and moor.

No man could support himself, his wife and his children on the produce of such a holding. And that, in fact, was the intention. To feed their families and pay their generally exorbitant rents, as landowners knew very well, crofters would require employment outside the comparatively limited range of agricultural activities which had been sufficient for their non-crofting predecessors. And the only such employment available, of course, was in the kelp industry.

From the point of view of Lord Macdonald and his fellow landowners, then, the crofting system was a beautifully efficient form of exploitation. By limiting the amount of land at the family's disposal, by charging a high rent for that land and by paying extremely low prices for kelp, island lairds provided themselves with a workforce which was as much at their mercy, and as firmly under their control, as any set of slaves on a colonial plantation. The slaves, indeed, may have been rather better off. Compared to the condition of the average crofter, wrote one early nineteenth-century traveller in the Highlands and Islands, 'The state of our negroes is paradise'. And it is not at all surprising, therefore, that island people responded unfavourably to the way in which their landlords now expected them to live.

*   *   *

Sir Alexander Macdonald of Sleat, that old Etonian about whom both Boswell and Johnson were so unkind, had rounded off his family's anglicisation by obtaining the title of Lord Macdonald and by marrying Elizabeth Diana Bosville, heiress to various rich lands in Yorkshire. Their son, also Alexander, who inherited his father's Skye estates in 1795, was thus wholly removed from the Gaelic background and sympathies of his ancestors. And between the second Lord Macdonald and his tenants there seems to have been, in the end, no emotional bond save that of mutual incomprehension and antipathy.

He had 'no objection', the new laird soon made known, to 'one or two sheep farms on a proper scale'. Nor had he any objection to utilising his consequently

Fish nets, Dunvegan pier.

displaced tenants in the rapidly expanding kelp business. 'The soil is not only to be tilled,' concluded a 1799 report on the Macdonald properties, 'but from the surrounding ocean, and its rocky shores, immense sums may be drawn. As these funds are inexhaustible, the greater the number of hands employed so much more will be the amount of produce arising from their labour.' This was not to say, of course, that these 'hands' should be well treated. On the contrary, the miniscule crofts set aside for them were to be located, as Lord Macdonald's advisers observed, 'in the least profitable parts of the estate' where they would 'not interfere with, or mar, the laying out of better farms'.

And so there began the first of the island's many clearances. In 1801 alone, notices of eviction were issued to 267 of Lord Macdonald's Skye tenants. And in the Macdonald estate records, now preserved in Edinburgh, there can be seen the roughly worded petitions which some of these tenants forwarded to Lord Macdonald in the naïve, though strangely touching, belief that he was still their chief and, as such, would stand by them in their time of trouble.

Their great-great grandfathers had fought and died beside his great-grand uncle at the Battle of Killiecrankie. And on innumerable winter evenings they had heard old men recite the names and exploits of his remoter ancestors: Donald Gorm Og, Donald Gorm Mor, Donald Gruamach and all the others who linked him with Clan Donald's heroic past; with fourteenth and fifteenth century Lords of the Isles and, ultimately, with the great Somerled himself. But Alexander Macdonald, tenth baronet and second lord, was not of the

Gaelic world still inhabited by the people who now pleaded with him. Their petitions were bundled up, folded away and forgotten about. And they themselves were ejected from their homes.

Having been thus removed from land which their families had occupied for generations, Lord Macdonald's tenants did not see why they should tamely acquiesce in his plans for them. A passage to America could then be bought cheaply. And either the United States or British North America were surely to be preferred to the miserable crofts to which Lord Macdonald was sending them. 'Let us go and may God's blessing be with us,' runs one song composed by such an emigrant. 'Let us go and charter a vessel. Better that than to remain under landlords who will not tolerate tenantry.' In America, it was said, 'they were not troubled with landlords or factors'. In America, a man, however humble, might get a farm of his own. In America, it seemed, 'all the people were happy and on an equal footing and there were no rents paid there'. From Prince Edward Island on the Gulf of the St Lawrence, the Gaelic bard Malcolm Buchanan, Calum Ban MacBhannain, who came originally from Skye, instructed his former neighbours to follow his example. 'If you go over the sea,' the singer tells the listeners to his songs, 'bring my greetings to my friends. Urge them, without delay, to flee the rents and come out as soon as opportune for them. If they could find a time and means to come over they would not be beholden to Macdonald. This is the isle of contentment.'

There were many Skye people who took Calum Ban at his word. By the beginning of 1803, it was reported, no less than two thirds of all Lord Macdonald's tenants in Sleat were preparing to leave for North America. And though there would come a time when such emigration would be encouraged energetically by island landlords, that time was not yet. The second Lord Macdonald needed his crofters to make his kelp; for without his revenues from kelp his fortunes would be in complete disarray. And so the Sleat tenants had to be persuaded, or forced, to stay.

In April 1803, therefore, Lord Macdonald's factor was instructed 'to express' to the tenantry 'his lordship's regret that so many of the inhabitants have been seduced from their attachment to their native country'. Why this was so, Lord Macdonald professed himself at a loss to understand. His people had been 'invariably treated with kindness', he asserted. Their rents had not been increased as often as they might have been. And as for those individuals 'whom it was necessary to remove in the arrangement of some of the farms', they had no real cause for complaint; certainly they had no reason to embark for America, 'a remote and desolate part of the world', in Lord Macdonald's view. Families who had been asked to quit their former possessions were to be given new crofts, Lord Macdonald pointed out. And these crofts, he was convinced, would provide their occupiers with 'the means of living comfortably in their own country'.

Acknowledging privately that his assurances, by themselves, might not produce the desired results, Lord Macdonald also agreed to postpone a number of evictions and other charges — much to the displeasure of his factor who thought it 'beneath the dignity' of his employer 'to yield to a few restless,

Morning clouds over the Minch.

infatuated people'. By so yielding, however, Lord Macdonald bought time. That time he put to good use by co-operating with other Highland landlords in obtaining legislation which had the effect of so raising the cost of a transatlantic passage as to close that particular escape route from his estate. 'The emigration is entirely stopped now,' Lord Macdonald's factor wrote happily in the summer of 1803, 'from the Act of Parliament which puts it out of the poor people's power to pay the increase of freight'. Those who had not already gone were obliged to remain and made to accept the inadequate crofts which were again offered to them. Lord Macdonald's kelping income was thus guaranteed. And he begun to plan the new mansion which that income had made possible.

* * *

While kelp prices remained high, as they did for most of the nineteenth century's first twenty years, crofters retained their value to their landlords. Then alternative, and cheaper, sources of industrial alkali were discovered by southern manufacturers. The kelp boom ended. And the crofters to whom it had given employment were left with no resources except their crofts. On them they grew, with reckless determination, the one crop which their couple of hectares of generally indifferent land could produce in sufficient quantity to sustain a family. That crop was the potato. And when, in 1846, potato blight first reached northern Scotland, the island was necessarily plunged into famine.

In the northern part of Scotland, reported one of the relief agencies which were hurriedly established in Glasgow and Edinburgh with the aim of providing food for starving Highlanders, 'The potato is the principal produce of the ground under tillage and the principal article of food for the people. In the more eastern parts, the potato probably forms one half of the subsistence of the people; in the western districts, fully three-fourths; and in the islands it is the principle means of subsistence.' Throughout the Highlands and Islands, continued the authors of that particular report, 'the potato crop has this last year, with few exceptions, totally failed; and, by this great and mysterious calamity, three-fourths of the food of this vast population has at once been withdrawn from them. It must be conceived that the effect of this terrible visitation of providence must, in these circumstances, be both immediate and appalling.'

Just how appalling became clear on Christmas Day, 1846, when a deputation from one of the famine relief organisations reached the southern part of Skye. None of that locality's crofters, the deputation's leader informed his Edinburgh headquarters, had escaped the effects of hunger. Nor had they escaped the even more horrifying consequences of the scurvy, typhus and cholera which followed in hunger's wake. 'We found the condition of them miserable in the extreme,' the deputation's leader wrote, 'and every day, as they said, getting worse; their houses, or rather their hovels, the very pictures of destitution and hopeless suffering.' Typhoid was especially prevalent, it appeared, and in such dread was it held by the entire community that those families who contracted it were usually 'left to their fate by their neighbours'.

The deputation had investigated 'one most deplorable case' involving a family of seven persons who had been affected by typhus fever over a period of several weeks. 'The eldest of the children, a son of about nineteen years of age, had died just when his mother was beginning to get on foot. No one would enter the house with the coffin for the son's remains. It was left at the outside of the door and the enfeebled parent and a little girl, the only other member of the family on foot, were obliged to drag the body to the door and put it in the coffin there, whence it was carried by a few of the neighbours, with fear and alarm, to its last resting place'.

His colleagues had declined to enter the 'wretched house', the deputation's spokesman went on. But he himself had insisted on so doing. 'I found the father lying on the floor,' he said, 'on a wisp of dirty straw, the bedclothes, or rather rags of blanket, as black nearly as soot, his face and hands of the same colour, never probably having been washed since he was laid down. The whole aspect of the man, with his hollow features and sunken eyes, and his situation altogether, was such as I had never beheld before. In a miserable closet, beyond the kitchen where the father lay, I found the rest of the family, four daughters from about eleven years of age to seventeen, all crammed into one small bed, two at one end and one at the other; the rags of blanket covering them worse, if possible, than those on the father; their faces and persons equally dirty, the two youngest having no night clothes of any kind. One of those poor girls was very ill and was not likely to recover. The others had the fever more mildly but had not been so long in it. The effluvia and stench in this place, and indeed in

Path to the Black Rock, Portree.

Talisker Bay.

Byre at Glasphein, Staffin.

The Black Memorial Church, Portree.

every part of the miserable dwelling, were such that I felt I could not remain long without great risk of infection as there was no means of ventilation and not even of light. The poor woman said she had got a stone or two of meal, she did not know from whom, which had barely served to make gruel for the unfortunate patients. The family had no means whatsoever of their own.'

From other parts of the island there came equally harrowing descriptions of people forced to eat roots and seaweed in a desperate attempt to keep themselves alive; of fields from which there emanated the inescapable stench of rotting potatoes; of children with strangely protruding bellies and peculiarly swollen and deformed limbs; of scenes, in short, which have been made too familiar in our own time by television pictures of famine in Africa.

Then the hunger and the suffering were nearer home; for in that bleak and bitter winter of frequent snows and blizzards, the people of the island experienced adversity of a kind for which not even the clearances of previous years had prepared them. 'At the appointed time and place,' wrote one witness of the emergency food distributions organised in Skye by the relief agencies, 'the poor creatures troop down in hundreds, wretched and thin, starved and wan. Some have clothing, some almost none and some are a mass of rags. Old and young, feeble and infirm, they take their stations and await their turn. Not a murmur, not a clamour, not a word; but they wept aloud as they told of their miseries.'

A sum equivalent to many millions of pounds, at today's values, was raised in southern cities and spent on oatmeal for Highland famine victims. Government aid was also provided and a naval ship was stationed off Portree to serve as an emergency supplies depot. One Skye laird, MacLeod of MacLeod, saved thousands of people by providing work and wages for them. More typical of the landowning fraternity's reaction to the crisis, however, was the conduct of the fourth Lord Macdonald.

The Macdonald estates were estimated to contain a destitute population of some 14,000. Prompted by the army officers who had taken charge of the government's relief programme in Skye, Lord Macdonald agreed to employ about 400 of them on a publicly funded drainage project. To the dismay of the hard-pressed military men, this particular scheme was abandoned within weeks of its commencement.

Macdonald's factor then bought a cargo of meal in Liverpool. But meal prices were rising almost daily that winter and, instead of shipping their newly acquired foodstuffs to Skye, the estate management resold them in the south where, it was reported, 'a handsome profit' was made on the transaction. The upshot, as one disgusted official commented, was that Lord Macdonald, by refusing to do anything to alleviate his tenants' plight, was effectively compelling starving crofters to travel 'every week' to the naval meal stores at Portree, 'often distances of thirty or forty miles from the extreme parts of the island, to procure the food which neither he nor his factor would import for them'.

The famine was not without its impact on the thinking of the men in charge of the Macdonald properties, however. It proved conclusively, as far as they were concerned, that their crofting tenants had become a cause of trouble rather than a source of income. Since there was no longer any demand for kelp, there was no further need for crofters. And so the people whom the Macdonald estate management had once been so determined to retain in Skye were now to be turned off their holdings and shipped abroad. It would be 'of immense advantage', opined Lord Macdonald's factor, if his lordship were to take the lead in 'encouraging the system of clearing croft farms'. His lordship was happy to oblige; and there followed a new round of evictions which, in the words of the then parish minister of Sleat, were 'attended with circumstances of heartless cruelty'.

One of the many sheep farms created in the course of these clearances which occurred in the years around 1850, was afterwards described, by an agricultural surveyor, as 'superior'. Its arable land, said to be of 'fair quality', extended to 183 acres. A further 2761 acres of 'good quality' pasture were also available. For such an attractive holding, Lord Macdonald naturally expected, and duly obtained, a very good rent. And since this single rent was considerably higher than the total rent paid by the crofters who had formerly occupied the land in question, Lord Macdonald no doubt thought their removal more than justified, from a purely economic perspective at any rate.

Despite these financial gains, one might have expected the farm's name to have been changed by the people responsible for the forcible ejection of its previous incumbents; the more so since that name had become synonymous with unrelenting harshness. But Lord Macdonald and his estate managers

Drying peat, Penifiler.

Roofscape, Portree.

Misty morning over Portree.

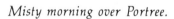

Glamaig.

were not given to such gestures. On their ledgers, and in their accounts, those 183 acres of arable and 2761 acres of pasture continued to be entered as Boreraig and Suisnish; places which are to be reached, you may recall, by way of the track that starts at Camas Malag.

* * *

'When I look back now from this high hill of my old age,' said Black Elk of the Oglala Sioux, remembering the white men's massacre of his tribe, 'I can still see the butchered women and children lying heaped and scattered all along the crooked gulch as plain as when I saw them with eyes still young. And I can see that something else died there in the bloody mud and was buried in the blizzard. A people's dream died there. The nation's hoop is broken and scattered and the sacred tree is dead.'

And what was true of North America's native peoples was true also of the island's Gaels. They, too, were thought by all men in authority to be obstructing the advance of something that these same men called progress. And as happened to the Oglala Sioux, as happened to so many others in so many different parts of the world, their lands were taken from them and given to strangers. In the phrase that Skye people used to describe the annihilation of their communities, the fires in their houses were put out. And with the extinguishing of these fires, which had been kept burning day and night for generations, another sort of continuity was ended. The links that bound the present to the past were severed one by one and a culture which had endured for centuries was soon left as rootless as the people to whom it belonged. In the world that had been remade to suit the tastes of men like Lord Macdonald, it seemed, there was no room for either Gaels or Gaelic. 'It is not surprising,' said one bard of that terrible time, 'that the sweet mother tongue should die; the deer in the wilderness do not speak and the white sheep have no language.'

Such was the great sadness of the clearances. Not only did they inflict hardship on the many for the profit of the few; they also snuffed out much of the unrealised potential of this little civilisation on the north-western edge of Europe. And that has left us all the poorer.

For some 1500 years — ever since Christianity was brought to the island by Columba, Moluag, Maelrubha and the other Gaelic-speaking monks from Ulster who are commemorated still in Skye placenames — the island had been part of a wider Celtic commonwealth which included, at its greatest extent, all of Ireland and almost all of Scotland. And in the townships obliterated by last century's lairds there survived something of that commonwealth's finest accomplishments: the ancient sagas featuring Cuchullain, Diarmid, Osgar, Deirdre and the rest of Gaeldom's prechristian warriors, heroes and heroines; the songs, the music, the poetry and the stories of a more recent period; above all, a way of assessing the world and humanity's place in it which owed little or nothing to those philosophies employed to rationalise the avarice and ruthlessness so characteristic of the southern society that was said, by practically everyone of any consequence, to be Gaeldom's superior as well as Gaeldom's conqueror.

Waterfall, Allt Mhic Mhoirein.

Morning mist: the Cuillin from Portree.

The Cuillin from Bayfield.

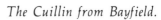

The road to Braes.

The Gaels had finally absorbed the Vikings who did so much to threaten the achievements of the uniquely Celtic form of Christianity which flourished here at a time when most of England, and most of continental Europe, had relapsed into paganism. In the Lordship of the Isles they had created, in the middle ages, a Gaelic principality which safeguarded Gaeldom's integrity when the Scottish kingdom, itself founded by Gaels, became so anglicised as to regard Gaelic-speakers as little better than barbarians and infidels.

But the lordship was eventually overthrown and, in its absence, Skye and the rest of Gaeldom could no longer be protected against the repeated attacks mounted, from the sixteenth century onwards, by successive governments in Edinburgh and London. At first these external onslaughts had foundered on a united community in which chief and clansman adhered to the same values, shared the same objectives and went to war in the same cause. That solidarity did not endure, however. And of all the things that made the clearances so dreadful, none was more demoralising in its implications than the fact that the dispossessions were ordered by men descended from the traditional leaders of the society they now destroyed.

'Look around you,' runs one poetic condemnation of the Macdonald laird visited by Johnson and Boswell, 'and see the nobles with no pity for miserable ones, with no kindness to kinsmen. They are of the opinion that you are not of the land.' And in putting that opinion into effect, the new style landowners betrayed, as well as drove out, their own people. 'They have lost their sight of every law and promise,' lamented the bard John MacCodrum, 'that was among the people who took this land from the enemy.'

In Skye, as in the faraway places remembered by Black Elk, a people had been broken and a way of life abruptly terminated. The mountain, said another bard, was now 'a wilderness with no tillage on its face'; and 'very chill' was the view from the pass: 'There is many a poor hut levelled, a green site on every side; where the fire and the children were, the rushes grow the highest.' Perhaps it makes little sense to regret these things and to believe that there should have been a better way. But Skye, I'm afraid, tends to engender such emotions.

6

A COUPLE of kilometres to the south of the Sleat township of Isle Ornsay, in a former shepherd's house at a place called Braigh an Uird, Ruairidh Hamilton, aged four, is one of a dozen children attending the Wednesday morning session of the playgroup organised by Anne MacAskill from Breakish. Anne is helping Ruairidh make a sandcastle and they are conversing all the time in Gaelic. It is one of the playgroup's rules that all adult helpers speak to the children in that language; the playgroup exists, in fact, to promote its use among the island's youngest age group. But in Ruairidh's case, Anne has no alternative. Not very long ago there were thousands of Skye people who understood little or no English. Now there are just a handful, all of them children. And Ruairidh Hamilton is one.

When he goes to school, Ruairidh will not be strapped, as my own grandfather was, should he have the temerity to reply to his teacher in Gaelic. But he, too, will be taught entirely in English. And because there are now fewer than 80,000 Gaelic speakers in this country of some 55 million people, he will be necessarily and ceaselessly exposed to the majority language from which he has so far been shielded by parents committed, well beyond the common run of folk, to the preservation of a form of speech of which most Britons have never heard a word.

Although the funds available to Gaelic are still pathetically inadequate, there are now more Gaelic broadcasts and more Gaelic books than there have ever been before. This I welcome unreservedly. But I also find it hard to shed a dire conviction that all the varied efforts being made on the language's behalf have about them something of the nature of spitting in the wind. Anne MacAskill's playgroup, and others like it, are intended to associate Gaelic with the fun and enjoyment which, on children's television and elsewhere, are so firmly linked with English. But it is noticeable that, with one or two exceptions, the children whom she addresses in Gaelic invariably respond in English. 'They understand Gaelic alright,' she says. 'But they almost all refuse to speak it. Why that is I just don't know.'

The Cuillin from the Meall, Portree.

Lobster boat at Bayfield, Portree.

The Red Cuillin from Loch Ainort.

And how do you explain why all this matters so very very much? If you are, for instance, a Gaelic poet whose audience is inevitably limited to the poetry-reading minority of that Gaelic-speaking minority of under 80,000 individuals, how do you convey to someone secure in his or her membership of the English language community, numbered now in hundreds of millions worldwide, the sickening sense of solitude that stems from your role as custodian of a culture which seems destined to die within two or three more generations?

Suppose, I once said to a group of conservationists and naturalists who had asked me to talk to them about the Hebrides, suppose that English had somehow become confined to a handful of people in a hilly corner of Cumbria. Suppose that the language of Chaucer, of Shakespeare, of Milton, of Dickens, of Cromwell and of Churchill was about to become extinct. Would you, too, not feel that you were about to be deprived of something precious?

But the thing was so far-fetched as to be meaningless. 'Well, yes, it would be nice if we could keep Gaelic going,' remarked one Englishman. 'But you could have said the same thing about Latin. You're just romancing really. I'm afraid the world's no longer going your way.'

'But that was exactly where he was wrong,' says Gaelic playwright Norman Macdonald when I tell him this story in his home at Kensaleyre. 'The world *is* going our way. That's what gives me encouragement. Everywhere you look there is a new emphasis on the importance of the small community. There's a new determination to work with nature, not against it. There's a growing disenchantment with the huge, unwieldy, thoughtless, feelingless cultures that have dominated the world for the last two hundred years.

'The Gaelic psyche is in tune with this shift of opinion. We have never lost our regard for nature. It's not us who are out there in these huge purse-seine trawlers emptying the seas of fish. No Gael could possibly go along with industrial fishing, I believe. No Gael could see the sense in killing millions of fish in order to produce fishmeal in order to feed the fishmeal to cattle in order to have more steaks. That sort of terrible destructiveness is just not in the Gael.

'More and more people are questioning these things. More and more people want to change these things. And Gaelic will be swept along on that tide. It will survive because it's got to survive, because of what it can contribute to the world. We have to tell people about this culture of ours. We have to interpret it to the world, give the world access to our songs, our music, our way of thinking.

'Our poets alone have made that essential. The reservoir of poetry that we have in Gaelic is so important to humanity that we just can't let the language die. Of course that poetry will be there in books as long as we have books. But if there are no Gaels, if there are no places where people talk and joke and swear in Gaelic every day, it will not be appreciated. To get properly to grips with poetry, you have to have not just the learned language but the language that you get, as they say, at your mother's knee. You have to have the language in your bones.

'What we need most of all is confidence in ourselves. That's what we haven't had for long enough. And it's their confidence I most envy about the English. Go and visit one of these little villages in the southern part of England. And then go and have a look at its churchyard. There will be gravestones there that are almost a thousand years old. Compare that incredible continuity, that tremendous security, with what's happened to the Gaels. Not a family among us wasn't dispossessed and pushed around and uprooted by the clearances. No wonder that we lost belief in our importance.'

*   *   *

Restoring that missing self-esteem is the primary purpose of Sabhal Mor Ostaig, Skye's Gaelic College, in the south-eastern corner of Sleat. Sabhal Mor means simply the great barn for this squat, foursquare and powerful building was one of those put up when the second Lord Macdonald was removing his clansmen to make way for big farms of the sort that required prestigious accommodation of this type. But these farms were not the financial success that they were meant to be. And in the 1970s, when the last of the Macdonald lands were sold, the Sabhal Mor was derelict. Now it is Scottish Gaeldom's first centre of higher education since the collapse of the medieval Lordship of the Isles; a place where a determined and energetic effort is being made to reverse the thrust of those educational policies which, for so long, have had so debilitating an effect on places like the island.

In the schools which the state provided for us in the Highlands and Islands, we learned nothing of our own heritage and background. The history that we

Norman Macdonald.

Winter's morning, Bayfield, Portree.

Skyscape from Aird Bhearnasdail.

The Cuillin from Elgol.

were taught was the history of England, not the history of Scotland, and most certainly not the history of what had happened to our own localities. The poetry that we were made to read was English poetry. The music that we heard was not our music. We were told nothing of land use, of agriculture, forestry or fishing. At each and every turn, we were directed away from our own communities and encouraged to accept that, wherever our future lay, it did not lie at home. If we wanted to get on, it was assumed, then we had better begin by getting out.

For a century or more, the island's major export has been its best people. No book about Skye is complete without its list of famous Skyemen, not one of whom achieved his fame in his own place. And when I visit a Skye croft and when, on the mantelpiece and on the sideboard, I see the graduation photographs of men and women now working in Inverness and Edinburgh, in London, in Montreal, Toronto, Washington and San Francisco, I am continually tantalised by the thought of how they could have altered their own island for the better if only they could have made their own lives in the villages where their parents are now growing old.

Even worse than this sending away of talented individuals has been the insidious devaluing of those who have remained. When people are made to believe that their culture, their language and, indeed, their entire way of life are, in some sense, inferior and second-rate, then these people will be necessarily lacking in self-confidence. And lacking self-confidence, they will also be deprived of initiative and enterprise. Instructed that their communities have nothing to offer them, they will come to believe that themselves. They will come to think that the decline and the decay they see around them are as unalterable as the weather. And they will not have the spirit to begin to put things right.

Like Anne MacAskill's playgroup, Sabhal Mor Ostaig is intended to change all that. Here students are taught entirely in Gaelic. Here they study the Highlands and Islands, past and present, as well as learning something of the experience of comparable regions elsewhere: the west of Ireland, Brittany, the northern part of Norway, the Faroe Islands, Iceland and Canada's maritime provinces. And here, still more significantly, they are taught economics, accountancy, computing and all the other skills required for the management of a business in an island setting. For the Sabhal Mor course, in the words of the feasibility study which preceded its inauguration in 1983, is intended to educate people for a role in a rural Highland or Hebridean community rather than to train them for professions in the cities'. And that amounts, quite literally, to a revolution.

It is, I think, appropriate that the man presiding over this remarkable experiment is a product of the other surviving segment of the Gaelic world. Sabhal Mor's principal, Sean O'Drisceoil, comes from Kilkenny and, before moving to Skye, he worked in Donegal. 'Young people here have traditionally been taught in a very academic way and have had to leave the island to get both a higher education and a job that makes use of that education,' he says. 'Not only have these people been lost to their own communities. Others with the

Sabhal Mor's principal, Sean O'Drisceoil.

necessary commercial expertise have had to be imported when business opportunities have occurred. We want these opportunities to be taken up by local people who have had the benefit of the sort of training that this college is providing.'

For Sabhal Mor Ostaig's senior lecturer, John Norman MacLeod, who comes originally from Staffin in the northern part of Skye, his move here was something of an act of faith. Like college secretary Norman Gillies, also from Staffin, he gave up a secure job on the mainland to participate in a venture which, John Norman admits, was regarded initially with an awful lot of scepticism. 'We didn't know if we'd get enough students,' he says. 'Funding was, and still is, a major anxiety. The books and teaching materials that we needed just didn't exist. It hasn't been easy. It isn't easy now. But it's certainly been worth while.'

I meet Sabhal Mor's students to discuss the prospects for crofting. We argue the issue, back and forth, for a couple of hours. We talk about the way the land ought to be worked, the way that crofting should be financed, the probable impact on the island of likely alterations in the Common Market's agricultural policy. In the end, we have not changed the world. But we have had a detailed debate about the sort of vital local issue on which islanders like these students were not previously encouraged to have considered views of any kind. That such should ever have been the case will seem, to Sabhal Mor Ostaig's graduates, quite inexplicable. And that is a measure of the college's accomplishment.

Poles for drying salmon nets, Invertote.

Ben Tianavaig from Braes.

The Cuillin from Glen More.

That evening, in Sabhal Mor Ostaig's large and well-appointed hall, Sleat's local history society, Comunn Eachdraidh Shleibhte, is meeting. One of several such associations in Skye, its purpose is to assist islanders to explore their past by way of their own recollections and memories and stories. Some such sessions, says the society's chairman, Duncan MacInnes, have attracted as many as fifty people. And that is one more indication, he believes, of the emergence of a new pride in Skye's identity.

At the meeting's end, I pause to speak to a group of people at the door. They switch from Gaelic to English as I approach and I am reminded, as I always am at Sabhal Mor, of a comment made by the Irish novelist James Plunkett, following a similar experience in Dingle, County Kerry. 'I felt,' Plunkett wrote, 'that before I die I will speak my native language adequately enough to talk with those of my countrymen who have had it from birth, so that they won't shame me by having to change to English on my account.'

*   *   *

I was first shown around Sabhal Mor Ostaig in the mid-1970s by Iain Noble who owns the land on which the college stands. A businessman and merchant banker who belongs to an established landowning family in Argyll, Iain bought his extensive Skye properties from the present Lord Macdonald in 1972 with the aim of making them the focus of an entirely novel experiment in estate management.

'I had never been able to see why the West Highlands and Islands should be less prosperous than comparable places elsewhere,' Iain Noble says. 'I wanted to get to grips with the causes of the region's problems. I wanted to try and break the momentum of decline, the momentum that results from the young people going away and the old people becoming increasingly convinced that nothing can be done to stop their community slipping deeper and deeper into decline.

'I had been to Faroe and I had seen there an island community that was flourishing both economically and culturally. Faroe and Skye, I discovered, had had a roughly equivalent population at the beginning of this century. Now Faroe, for all its remoteness, has five or six times more people than we have. And there seems to me to be no real reason why we should not be doing every bit as well.

'The Gaelic language, I have always thought, is the key to everything else. Their revival of their language some forty years ago started the Faroese on the upward path. And I was convinced when I came here, as I'm still convinced, that the revitalisation of Gaelic would do the same for Skye and other parts of the Highlands and Islands. A community where a language is dying cannot possibly be a confident and expanding community. People who believe in their language and culture, on the other hand, will also believe in themselves. That's why we need places like Sabhal Mor Ostaig. And that's why we need Gaelic playgroups and Gaelic schools.'

Most of the many private estates in this part of Scotland are run on strictly

Isle Ornsay Lighthouse.

The Quirang.

Gable end, Luib.

Tote from Skeabost.

traditional lines: a bit of farming possibly; a little forestry perhaps; certainly some stalking. Iain Noble's estate is different in that its range of activities is much more extensive. In addition to a farm and a fish farm, the enterprises controlled from the estate office at Eilean Iarmain include a trading company, an hotel, a knitwear business and a whisky marketing concern. The estate's annual turnover has increased in under fifteen years from some £20,000 to about £1 million. The complement of full-time employees is now approaching forty. And Sleat, on which Iain Noble's estate is centred, has a more bustling air than most other parts of the island. Its school roll has grown from 22 to 70 in the last ten years. And there are many more young people living in the place.

'It has not been easy,' Iain Noble admits. Profits have been negligible or non-existent. And though Iain is convinced that the break-even point is now in sight, he describes the commercial aspects of his Skye involvement as 'a long, long haul'.

So why does he continue; why does he not abandon the island for Edinburgh where he still has banking interests and where, beyond doubt, he could make a lot more money? There are times when he has been disheartened by the difficulties he has encountered in Skye, he concedes. 'But I have always believed that I am doing something useful here,' he insists. 'I feel that I am doing a job that desperately needs to be done. And by being here I've also made many very valuable friends among people whom I would not have even met had I stayed in the south.'

Iain Noble is by no means universally popular in Skye. Such is the island's history, that all landowners are automatically suspect. And one who sets so much store by Gaelic and by job creation is, in a paradoxical sort of way, more suspect than the rest. 'Anyone who wants to change things is bound to be controversial and bound to offend,' Iain Noble acknowledges. 'And I want to change so many things. To me the solutions to our problems in the island seem so obvious. And maybe I'm inclined to get too far ahead of other people.'

On the evening that we meet to discuss his accomplishments, Iain Noble tells me about his latest plans for his estate. They seem to me to be far-fetched. But then, more than ten years ago, when he took me to inspect a set of dilapidated barns, byres and outbuildings and told me that they would one day be a place where islanders would be provided with a higher education in their own language, I refused to believe him. Now the Gaelic College, which began as one of Iain Noble's dreams, is a reality. And I no longer make the mistake of ever underestimating this most complex and most untypical island laird.

7

IN Glen Brittle this November morning the only sound is that of water falling far away. A little patch of cloud, moving steadily south-westwards, brushes across the higher peaks. But the north-easterly breeze that is clearly blowing on the Cuillin ridge is absent here in the shelter of the hills. Although it is wearing on towards midday, the quiet, windless glen is in deep shadow under a predominantly clear sky. There are no signs of any slackening in the overnight frost. The sun, even at its highest, will remain hidden. Only the upper reaches of Sgurr na Bhairnich are catching its rays. A little further to the west, the darkly shaded recesses of Coir' an' Tairnailear and Coir' a' Mhadaidh will be denied even the slightest warmth. The marbling of snow in their north-facing gullies will persist into the spring.

The sharply ascending road out of the glen bears away north-westwards towards Carbost. Here, too, the day is peculiarly still. Birds can be heard calling intermittently from the weed-covered mud and shingle at the head of Loch Harport. Down there, near the spot where the River Drynoch enters the sea and where the consequently brackish water is more inclined to freeze, the shore is fringed by a white, paperlike layer of ice left high and dry by the receding tide.

All around the slanting sun picks out the long, low corrugations of last century's lazybeds. Those on the smooth, steep hillside called Braighe Coille na Droighniche are reflected on the rippleless surface of the loch. There are more above Drynoch itself and more still above Satran and Merkadale. It is as if some giant from Gaelic mythology had come striding down from the mountains and, enormous rake in hand, had set about constructing a seedbed on a scale proportionate to his stature.

At a place called Grunagary, to the west of the Vikisgill Burn, I pause to examine these earth markings at closer quarters. Each flattened ridge is two to three metres wide and perhaps half a metre high. This particular cluster is enclosed by a turf dyke and its parallel undulations, as a result, are comparatively short. On the opposite side of the valley, however, are some

The Quirang.

which are several hundred metres long. And similar conglomerations are to be seen not just in the general vicinity of Loch Harport, though there they are particularly evident, but in practically every corner of the island.

On the other side of the Minch, on the rocky eastern seaboard of Harris, such lazybeds are still in use. And to Frank Fraser Darling, ecologist and agriculturalist, they seemed, in the 1940s, to be symbolic of the intricate and painstaking fashion in which crofters were obliged to make the most of their meagre scraps of land. 'Nothing can be more moving to the sensitive observer of Hebridean life,' wrote Fraser Darling, 'than these lazybeds of the Bays district of Harris. Some are no bigger than a dining table, and possibly the same height from the rock, carefully built up with turves and with the seaweed carried there in creels by women and girls. One of these tiny lazybeds will yield a sheaf of oats or a bucket of potatoes, a harvest no man should despise.'

Here in Skye, too, the same techniques were employed to raise crops on hard or waterlogged ground which otherwise would have been barren. And despite the apparently deprecatory implications of their English designation, the resulting lazybeds, or *feannagan*, 'speak to not a little labour', as was remarked by one nineteenth-century visitor to the island, on the part of the people responsible for their formation.

Lazybeds were made with the help of nothing more sophisticated than spade or mattock. A likely looking site was selected. A trench was taken out. Half of the excavated material was heaped up on one side, half on the other. A second trench or ditch, to the left or right of the first, resulted in a substantial

Drynoch: evidence of lazybeds.

mound between the two. And this process was then repeated more or less indefinitely. The initial effect of these excavations on an island hillside such as Braighe Coille na Droighniche would have resembled nothing so much as the preparations now made for commercial tree planting. And though modern forestry companies use caterpillar tractors and heavy steel ploughs to break in marginal land, their intentions are the same as those of last century's crofters: to improve soil drainage and to provide themselves with relatively dry strips of ground on which something other than rushes and heather can be grown.

Especially after the greater part of their pasture land had been taken away from them and added to the sheep farms favoured by their landlords, these lazybeds kept many crofting families alive; providing them with food which otherwise would not have been obtainable. And as I press on from Drynoch, through Meadale and Sumardale to Bracadale, I come across more remnants of them: mute monuments, in this now largely empty quarter of the island, to habitations long since swept away.

* * *

Places like Bracadale, Sumardale and Meadale, as is indicated still by their pronunciation, were once settled by Vikings. A thousand years or more ago, these men from Norway's western coast would have swung their longships around Idrigill Point and, probing carefully beyond Wiay and Oronsay, islands which also bear distinctively Scandinavian names, they would have beached their sea-battered craft eventually at the entrances to the green valleys where they were to farm and where they were to make their homes.

Later these same valleys came under the sway of the MacLeods of Dunvegan, Gaelic-speaking chieftains who, like many of their clansmen, were themselves of Norse descent and whose seagoing galleys were modelled on the longships of their Norwegian forebears. Later still, other MacLeods, landlords now instead of chiefs, individuals who preferred English to Gaelic and who also preferred, as was said caustically, sheep to men, were to rid their estates of the people whose long neglected lazybeds are being swallowed up now by the rough, rank vegetation these same lazybeds were intended to displace.

Indeed, it was here in the little villages around Loch Bracadale — in places like Roag and Vatten and Harlosh and Ullinish and Struan — that it first became evident, as early as 1739, that the MacLeods of Dunvegan were no longer to be trusted to put the age-old obligations of kinship before the newer, and less intangible, dictates of financial self-interest.

On an October afternoon that year, a ship put into Loch Bracadale. As her anchor was let go and her sails furled, any onlookers on the loch's well-populated eastern shore might have made out her name, *William*, on her bows. And as the day wore on towards evening, it may well have become known in the district that the visiting ship's master was one William Davison. Both he and his vessel, it would have been reported, belonged to Donaghadee in Ireland. And they had come to Skye, or so it was suggested, to put ashore a cargo of brandy and other liquor.

Salmon nets drying, Sconser.

Since the island gentry of the time were less than enthusiastic about paying customs dues on their imported spirits, this was a plausible enough story. However, William Davison's dealings with Skye's more eminent residents were not confined to a little mutually beneficial smuggling. He had much more lucrative business on hand; business which had its origins, or so it was subsequently claimed, in an agreement between Sir Alexander Macdonald of Sleat and Norman MacLeod of Dunvegan, the island's principal chieftains.

The purpose of that agreement, the two men afterwards insisted, was simply to devise a means of ridding Skye of thieves, robbers and other undesirables. And they had concluded, as Sir Alexander was to note in an anxious letter which he wrote to one of his legal advisers after this joint accord had got him into potentially serious trouble, that the 'best method' of attaining their objective 'was to get some clever fellow' to round up any known undesirables. Having thus been seized, these miscreants would, as Sir Alexander put it, be put 'on board a ship' which would then 'carry them over to the plantations'.

By the plantations, Sir Alexander meant Britain's North American colonies. And the 'clever fellow' who was to have the job of despatching any available criminals in that direction? Well, he turned out to be a certain Norman MacLeod of Bernera, one of the more important tenants of the Dunvegan chieftain. And it was at this Norman's invitation, in fact, that William Davison had brought his ship into Loch Bracadale.

William Davison, it seems likely, had needed little in the way of persuading. There was, at the time, good money to be made from exporting men and women to the American settlements. Workers were extremely scarce in places like the Carolinas. And planters there were prepared to pay high prices for so-called 'indentured labourers' — people whose status was virtually indistinguishable from that of slaves.

Thieves and other criminals were often transported in this way. But with the supply of such offenders constantly lagging far behind the New World demand for labour, the more unscrupulous practitioners of this unpleasant trade were in the habit of topping up their human cargoes from other sources. Not infrequently, it appears, they simply abducted their victims. It was as a result of suffering such a fate that, as the novel's title suggests, the young David Balfour came to be aboard the America-bound brig shipwrecked off Mull in the early chapters of Robert Louis Stevenson's *Kidnapped* — a tale inspired by well documented instances of this type of illegal seizure.

Norman MacLeod and William Davison, however, had much more ambitious plans than David Balfour's captors. They planned to offer for sale in America not one but scores of labourers and servants. And since it had been clear to them from the outset that the island was distinctly short of men and women who could be convincingly described as robbers or outlaws, they simply landed at night on the shores of Loch Bracadale where they descended on the surrounding homesteads and took as many prisoners as they could. They then crossed to Harris, also MacLeod territory, where they carried out a similar raid. And it was as a result of these activities that the *William* was soon under sail for Ireland with over 100 people, including 60 women and children, crammed in her holds.

Back in Donaghadee, Davison gave instructions for the *William* to be refitted for the Atlantic passage. The Skye and Harris people, meanwhile, he transferred to a couple of barns on the outskirts of the town. And it was from one of these barns, on the night of 4 November, 1739, that a number of the prisoners managed to escape into the surrounding countryside.

The fleeing islanders were pursued, retaken, bound hand and foot and promptly restored to the *William* where, by way of discouraging any further break-outs, they were beaten with cudgels and iron bars. The commotion caused by their bid for freedom, however, had attracted the attention of the authorities. Questions were asked. Inquiries were made. Soon the Donaghadee magistrates had ordered the release of the captives and had also issued warrants for the arrest of the unsavoury Captain Davison and his employer, the equally unappealing Norman MacLeod.

Both these wily birds, unfortunately, were found to have flown. And the latter, indeed, was soon back in Skye where his chief, far from returning him to Donaghadee to stand trial, permitted him to retain his tenancy and, a few years later, awarded him a much coveted commission in the local militia — all of which tends to confirm the prevalent contemporary opinion that both the MacLeod and Macdonald chieftains had had a hand in the entire operation which could hardly have taken place, after all, without their concurrence and from which, it was widely suspected, they hoped to derive some personal profit.

Neither chieftain, of course, was disposed to admit any complicity in the venture. While Sir Alexander put about his story of having merely wished to cleanse Skye of its malefactors, MacLeod of Dunvegan protested, equally unconvincingly, that 'we are entirely innocent of the crimes laid to our charge'. It would be best, he urged the government, to forget about the whole affair. Any prosecution, he added in a letter to a friendly politician, 'would be attended with a multitude of inconveniences' — not least because one of the probable accused, MacLeod himself, was then standing for parliament where, as he no doubt made clear to the responsible ministers in Edinburgh and London, he would, of course, be doing his best to further the interests of the governing party.

And so all the guilty men were permitted to go free. And though some at least of their intended plantation workers were to return to their homes in Bracadale, the entire episode was, in its callous disregard of traditional ties, a foretaste of what the future held in store for people like them. For if island chiefs were prepared to see their clansfolk sold, in effect, into slavery, they were most unlikely to feel any remorse about expelling these same clansfolk to make way for sheep.

Boreraig.

In 1826 and 1827 a total of at least 1300 people left the island for Nova Scotia and the other North American colonies. In the first of these years no fewer than 229 individuals from Bracadale, all of whom had received notices of eviction from their laird, MacLeod of Dunvegan, applied for government-assisted passages to Canada. In the early 1820s, Bracadale's population had passed the 2000 mark. Now it was plummeting. And the decrease, wrote the parish minister, was 'solely to be ascribed to the system of farming which has been adopted'. This system, he explained, consisted of 'throwing a number of farms' into one large holding and 'dispossessing and setting adrift the small tenants'.

It was at this time that the little valleys of Meadale and Sumardale, occupied continuously since at least the coming of the Norsemen whose names they bear, were forcibly depopulated. 'Meadale was first cleared,' Alexander MacAskill from Drynoch was to say some 40 years later, 'and I think there were ten or twelve families in it.' In Sumardale, he stated categorically, there were ten families: 'I myself remember these.' All of them, he continued, were removed from their possessions and these possessions, or holdings, were incorporated into a single sheep farm. As a result, said Alexander MacAskill, with understandable bitterness, 'all these townships are now vacant. There is not a creature there today.' Where had the Sumardale and Meadale people gone, he was asked. 'Many of them at that time,' he replied, 'went to America.'

* * *

On this November afternoon the last of the sun is finding its way into Meadale and glinting on the diminutive bay at the valley's foot. From overhead comes the grating call of a raven. And on the brae above the road, which is practically bereft of traffic, a man is whistling occasionally on his dog. He is surveying his sheep from a knoll that overlooks a broad sweep of hill and when I look back, from the better part of a kilometre down the Dunvegan road, he is still there, silhouetted against a frosty sky from which the light is steadily ebbing.

Along this road the Meadale people would have come one day in the 1820s; one more raggle-taggle band among the many then leaving the island for the last time. Each stone, each rock, each stream, each hillock would have been familiar to them. Each would have had its Gaelic name. Each would have featured in some story or legend long told in the township. On every one of these small and intimate landmarks the eyes of the older people, in particular, would have lingered and they would have felt the terrible sadness of knowing that all these familiar places were being left forever.

On they went, perhaps, past Beinn nan Lochan, past Glas Bheinn and Beinn Thuaithealain, past Coillore, Dun Garsin, Creag Dhubh, Ros a' Mheallain, on through the narrow cleft of Leacan Nighean an t-Siosalaich and then down across the moor by way of Glengrasco to Portree. And there, out in the bay, would have been moored a distinctively nineteenth-century successor to the *William* of Donaghadee: one of those grim and justifiably dreaded ships on which all aspiring emigrants were forced to take their chance.

Abandoned fishing boat.

One such vessel, the 400-ton *Frances Mary*, cleared St John, New Brunswick, on an icy morning in January, 1826. She was weighed down with timber from the great forests that stretched eastward into Upper Canada. And since she was one of scores of ships employed to transport the products of these forests to the booming market then provided by the shipyards on the Clyde and the Mersey, the *Frances Mary* left port largely unremarked. Such interest as was ever to attach to her was to be entirely posthumous; was to be the outcome, in fact, of the unusually gruesome circumstances surrounding her imminent demise.

The *Frances Mary*, it seems probable, was not a happy ship. Almost none of the craft participating in the Atlantic timber trade were in that highly selective category. For them to have been so, after all, would have been to defy the laws of commerce.

One of these laws, well understood in the 1820s at any rate, held that a vessel should be matched carefully with its cargo; with the most valuable commodities, logically enough, being entrusted to the soundest and best-equipped ships.

That was why, at the beginning of the nineteenth century, the finest vessels afloat were the so-called East Indiamen; large and stately craft with superb lines and lavish furnishings; their hulls constructed very often from the highest quality teak. In those ships the British East India Company transported the oriental spices and fabrics which were the basis of its fabled wealth and influence. And the company took the same care to ensure that its immensely precious cargoes reached their destinations as its successors were to display in entrusting their equally profitable consignments of China tea to the still-remembered clippers which were the East Indiamen's late nineteenth century successors.

But lumber, as the North Americans called the newly sawn planks and boards piled high on the unscrubbed decks of the *Frances Mary* that January day in 1826, was not in the same class as spices or tea. Lumber did not have to be kept completely free of seawater. Lumber did not have to arrive quickly. Lumber, ton for ton, was a lot less valuable than spices, tea, sugar, iron, coal — or, indeed, any other cargo that could be named. And though there was money to be made in shipping forest products, as more than one prosperous Glasgow family could have testified, the secret of doing well in the Atlantic timber business was to despatch as many cargoes as possible and at the lowest possible cost.

From a strictly financial perspective, then, there was no point in using good — and, therefore, expensive — ships to carry timber. And a United States *Dictionary of Commerce*, published in 1852, shrewdly and mercilessly summarised the consequently predominant characteristics of the vessels employed in the lumber business: 'It is well known that, generally speaking, they are of a very inferior class; it being the usual practice to turn worn out ships, unfit to carry dry cargoes, into this department.'

In British North America, too, these truths were evident. Of all the sailing ships afloat, said Canadians, the worst and the craziest 'came down' to lumber. Bought fourth-hand, fifth-hand and sixth-hand from owners who were surprised to learn that they were worth even the few guineas or dollars they received for them, such craft were not repaired because they were not worth repairing. And they were not insured because the cost of the insurance payments would soon have outstripped their meagre value.

Dirty, bedraggled, unpainted, her masts shortened to reduce the strains on her weakened, creaking hull, the typical timber ship was seldom more than a storm or two away from the bottom of the ocean.

So far gone, in fact, were many of these vessels that, when fully loaded, they were habitually held together only by means of a makeshift procedure known as 'swifting'. In recognition of their rotten state, chains were passed across their decks and under their keels in a desperate attempt to prevent their decrepit hulls flying apart under the pressure of the huge weights of timber thrust below their decks.

No worthwhile skipper would have put into the Atlantic in winter in such rickety craft. But the timber trade was also notorious for its almost total lack of skilled seamanship. Miserable, dangerous, semi-derelict ships inevitably attracted only those captains and crews who were so drunken, so incompetent, or both, that no other berths were available to them.

In such circumstances, disasters were as frequent as they were unavoidable. A good deal of the timber shipped out of St John and Quebec fetched up on Western Isles beaches — as did the corpses of the ill-paid misfits who had been engaged to convey that timber to the United Kingdom. Year in, year out, ship after ship was wrecked; sometimes as many as thirty or forty in a single season. And included in the tally for 1826 was the *Frances Mary*.

In March, two months after she had left St John, the *Frances Mary* was discovered in mid-Atlantic by a Royal Navy frigate. A dismasted, waterlogged hulk, she appeared — at first sight — to be completely lifeless. But the naval party sent to investigate were to return, clearly sickened and distressed, to report otherwise. There were a few survivors. They included two women. They had kept themselves alive by eating — raw — the livers and brains of fellow crew members who had already died.

But though the *Frances Mary* had been lost, other timber ships continued somehow to win through. Their Canadian lumber unloaded, work at once began on the crude conversion required by the nature of their return cargo. Inside dingy holds, still reeking of resin, rough decking was rapidly installed. On this decking there were elected tier after tier of eighteen-inch-wide wooden bunks; for holds that had been packed with timber on the eastward run would be equally congested westward bound: this time with emigrants from places like the island.

*   *   *

'Another load of poor emigrants is arrived in our harbour,' recorded Thomas Crawley, surveyor-general of Cape Breton Island, in September 1827. 'We know little of them yet,' Crawley continued, 'except that they

Fishing boats, Portree Bay.

brought with them some bad cases of malignant smallpox. Four are dead. Three more, I understand, are dying; and happy we shall be if the contagion does not spread over the country.'

Such were the hazards in store for the families then being expelled from Meadale. For the brig causing so much anxiety to Cape Breton's surveyor-general, the man primarily responsible for the governing of that extensive and then largely tree-covered island at the northern tip of Nova Scotia, was just the sort of vessel in which the Meadale people may have embarked. She was named *Stephen Wright*. Her voyage had begun in the Hebrides. It had ended in her anchoring off Sydney, Cape Breton's administrative centre, to report that of her 166 surviving passengers as many as 40 were seriously ill.

The harassed and overworked Crawley was perfectly willing to provide the brig's suffering occupants with both food and medical assistance. He was also determined, however, that Sydney's population should not be exposed unnecessarily to the epidemic that might follow an early landing by the emigrants aboard the *Stephen Wright*. His offer of aid, then, was conditional. It would be made available only if the smallpox victims remained exactly where they were.

This was not at all to the liking of the brig's master — 'an obstinate and brutish fellow', in the surveyor-general's opinion. The captain of the *Stephen Wright*, in fact, wished only to rid his ship of emigrants and be about his business. Whether his passengers lived or died, he made clear, was not his concern. 'The master,' Crawley was left to note despairingly, 'declares he will do nothing towards the relief or recovery of his unhappy living cargo and, in pursuance of that determination, perversely refuses to let air into the hold of the vessel where it must necessarily be pestilential.'

Such scenes were common enough in Cape Breton, a favoured destination for emigrants from the island, throughout the decade that brought the clearance of Meadale and Sumardale. 'In the course of the present year,' Sydney's magistrates would observe in 1828, 'upwards of 2100 persons have come into this district from the western part of Scotland.' Many of these incomers were from Skye. And a high proportion of them, as the Sydney magistrates reported, 'were quite destitute of food and also of the means of procuring it'. For them at least the New World held out no readily obtainable prospects of betterment.

Although Nova Scotia's administrators naturally complained about the expense and inconvenience entailed in their repeatedly having to provide financial and other help to half-starved emigrants from Skye and neighbouring islands, even those who were destitute were at least alive. That made them comparatively fortunate. In 1834 alone, more than 700 emigrants died in Atlantic shipwrecks. And in the six years between 1847 and 1853, when people were again pouring out of Skye, at least 59 emigrant ships were lost at sea.

An emigrant ship, after all, was simply a timber ship in another guise. And most timber ships, remember, were the dregs and dross of maritime commerce. To take passage in such a vessel was always to court catastrophe.

Coastal boulders, Score Bay.

Thousands of emigrants drowned. Thousands more died of disease; of smallpox, cholera, diphtheria, influenza, whooping cough, measles, pneumonia, typhus; even of persistent and chronic seasickness.

Little that was pleasant, then, awaited those confused and dejected refugees from Meadale as they clambered awkwardly aboard the ship which would, if they were lucky, convey them to Canada. Their voyage, made in the face of the Atlantic's prevailing westerly winds, might last for ten or even fifteen weeks. And when the weather was stormy, as it often was, the ship's hatches would be battened down and her passengers left to make what shift they might in the heaving, pitching gloom of the vessel's cold and streaming hold.

Down there, on narrow, congested and comfortless bunks, huddled the men, women and children whom MacLeod of Dunvegan — or MacLeod of MacLeod as he had taken to entitling himself — thought his estates well rid of. Down there, the space between each set of jerry-built decks was so slight that few adults could stand upright. Down there, hot food was unobtainable and water often bad. Down there, sanitary facilities were confined to a few easily spilled and frequently overflowing wooden buckets. Down there, seasickness was constant, the air foul and the stench so strong and appalling that emigrant ships could be detected, from a mile or two downwind, by their stomach-turning stink.

'I smell emigrant,' nineteenth-century Canadians were in the habit of remarking on encountering a skunk. But there was precious little humour in the conditions that produced the newly arrived settler's characteristic odour. These conditions, indeed, were commonly said, and occasionally proved, to be worse than those prevailing on the notorious vessels which transported slaves from Africa.

One such proof was provided in 1801. Two ships which sailed that year from the West Highlands for Nova Scotia were of such a size, it was reliably reported, that, had they been slavers putting out from the Gambia, they would have been permitted a combined cargo of 489 slaves. As it was, they carried 700 emigrants. And on one of these ships, not surprisingly, three out of every twenty people died.

No slaving skipper would have been inclined to risk such a death rate. His returns depended, to put the matter brutally, on the sale of his slaves in America. And the fitter and healthier these slaves were, the higher the price they fetched. Those families from Meadale, in contrast, paid their fares on embarking. And if they were to die in mid-ocean, well, that would save on the provision bill and make for a somewhat higher profit margin. It was little wonder, then, that many of those who left the island were never to see the Atlantic's other shore.

*   *   *

At the crest of the ridge between Meadale and Sumardale the breeze from the north blows coldly in my face. There are no lights in the darkening landscape. Hurrying on, I think of another evening spent some years ago in a place far from here; a place where a warm, dry wind, smelling of spruce trees, swirled down from the low, forested hills around a lake. Beside that lake there were plenty of lighted windows.

Earlier, driving along the road between the water and the woods, I had paid particular attention to the mailboxes at the end of the dusty dirt-tracks leading to the neat, white-painted homes where the lights were now coming on. Each mailbox bore its owner's surname. And every second surname was MacDonald or MacLeod.

In a car-filled field beside a wooden church a concert platform had been erected. Around it were hundreds of people, drinking iced beer from cans, eating popsicles and cotton candy, buying silvered balloons with Mickey Mouse motifs. On the platform a girl was singing. Her song was in Gaelic. It was about a place which she had never seen; a place she called *an t-eilean Sgitheanach*. That Cape Breton girl is separated from Meadale and Sumardale by seven or eight generations, by the better part of two whole centuries, by the entire width of the Atlantic Ocean. She would not wish to live here. And yet, in some strange way which neither she nor I can fathom, the island still, to her and others like her, remains home.

*   *   *

Outside Cape Breton Island and one or two other corners of Canada, that overseas attachment to Skye and the Scottish Highlands is now seldom

Stacan Gobhlach and Bagh Nan Gunnaichean looking towards the Outer Isles.

capable of expressing itself in Gaelic. And often the form it takes — the kilts, the plaids, the tartan tammies and the clan societies — seem more than a little bit absurd to those of us who are still on this side of the sea. And yet the fault, if there is any fault in this, is ours; for we have failed to meet the growing and sincere demand for information about Scotland with anything much more substantial than tourist brochures and the sort of songs that are an endless variant on *Granny's Hielan' Hame*. It is all the more ironic, then, that by far the most genuinely instructive of Skye's many tourist attractions has been financed largely by Americans.

The Clan Donald Lands Trust, in which Chicago businessman Ellice McDonald is the foremost figure, acquired Armadale Castle and the adjoining estate in the 1970s when it became evident that there would soon be no part of Skye left in the ownership of a Macdonald laird. The prospective absence of such a laird, I confess, was not a matter of great grief to me. Nor could I see why Americans, however rich, should squander their dollars on the restoration of a mansion built originally by a man who had evicted their own ancestors. Holding such views, I first visited the Clan Donald Centre in the refurbished Armadale Castle in the confident expectation of having all my prejudices confirmed; in the expectation, in fact, of being shown another collection of tatty relics of the type in which they specialise in other chieftainly residences round about. Instead I found the most thoroughly researched and best presented exhibition on Highlands and Islands history that I have ever seen.

And if that sounds like a gratuitous plug on behalf of Ellice MacDonald whom I do not know and whom I have never met, well, I feel I owe him something. Some years ago, he was instrumental in purchasing, on behalf of the Clan Donald Lands Trust, the extensive and invaluable manuscript records of the now defunct Macdonald estates. He intends, I believe, that these records will eventually be brought back from Edinburgh to Armadale. And for that all those of us with an interest in the island's past are truly in his debt.

8

IN Glen Drynoch and Glen Varragill, after dark, the moonlight makes a polished metal ribbon out of every river. But though the frost is hard in the late evening, there is a wide ring round the moon; the first sign of an impending breakdown in the weather. For accurate information about these things in Skye, you ignore those chatty characters from the London Weather Centre, where conditions in the home counties are of much more concern than the prospects for the northern half of Scotland; and you turn, instead, to the shipping forecast.

Outside, when I switch on the radio at half past midnight, there is scarcely any wind. But the announcer begins with warnings of gales in all northern and western sea areas, including Malin, Hebrides and Fair Isle. A rapidly deepening depression, she says, now some 300 miles west of Rockall, is expected to be over sea area Bailey in 24 hours time. Its central pressure will then be 960 millibars. And its fronts will be across the British Isles. Nor are the local details any more encouraging: 'Hebrides. South to south-east, four to five, increasing gale eight to storm ten; becoming south-west and increasing severe gale nine to violent storm eleven. Good, becoming moderate or poor. Fair at first, then rain.'

By next morning the barometer has fallen sharply. Dawn comes late and reluctantly, oozing greyly out of the east well after breakfast. Already the frost has gone and it is raining; at first, a sparse, sleety rain out of the south-east; soon, as the temperature lifts and the wind veers, a heavier downpour that batters on the windows in the rising gale.

When I leave the house in the early afternoon, the wind is whining through the outbuildings and heaving at the holly bushes by the gate. There is water everywhere. On the hillside opposite, white, rushing burns have appeared in places where there was no trace of them before. The roadside is awash. And water spurts and spouts from drains that only yesterday were dry.

In the city, rain falls usually from a matt grey sky that is glimpsed only between buildings. Here on the island, where the air contains no smoke or dirt and where the wind blows off the ocean, the clouds, even on days like this, are much more visible. Their jagged lower edges trail across the hills. And with the hills themselves to act as backdrops, the falling rain itself can be seen clearly. It does not come down evenly; but arranges itself in long, faint, streamer-like lines which are marched across the landscape by the storm.

In the lee of the house, it is dry. The rain passes overhead and is lashed along the road in rhythmic bursts. Out in the open, you try always to keep your back against the wind. The rain is painful in your face; it chills and stings and hurts your skin. And there are other inconveniences. In this sort of weather you get carefully into your car. If it is not pointing into the storm, its door may well be pulled from your hand and its door hinges buckled and twisted beyond repair.

At Drynoch the river is in spate. Its speed has the effect of smoothing out its usual waves and eddies and its peat-blackened waters, hurtling seawards, have a flat and oily look. Above Carbost there is the noise of falls which are the colour of coffee-stained cream. And at the eastern end of the rocky ridge known as Na Huranan, a hill burn has been turned back upon itself. Caught by the gale at the cliff's rim, its waters are being blown sharply upwards. Where there should have been a waterfall, there is only a ragged plume of smokey-seeming spray.

Samuel Johnson, who spent a day or two in Talisker towards the end of September, 1773, thought it 'the place beyond all that I have seen from which the gay and jovial seem utterly excluded'. He, too, came here in wild weather — 'almost one continued storm' — and his impressions were of 'lofty hills streaming with waterfalls' and 'a coast where no vessel lands but when it is driven by a storm on the rocks'.

Today there is just such a storm. Talisker is a flat-bottomed enclave in an otherwise unbroken chain of hills and cliffs. And the wind from the south-west bounces around inside it; so that the rain is pushed eastward along one side of the valley and then sucked back westward down the other. The effect, on looking down from Gleann Oraid, is of a sort of whirlpool.

There are high trees at Talisker and this afternoon even their trunks are being moved by the gale. At the shore, where the unobstructed wind is a steady, unrelenting thing, without the occasional lulls you get inland, the big, widely spaced waves follow one another in from the Minch and make you glad that you do not have to be out there on the sea.

In the evening, when I am driving from Portree towards Sligachan, the rain becomes so torrential that is its almost impossible to see through the silvery, flashing mass of falling water. The wind is even stronger and, above its sound, there is a sudden clap of thunder. Then, in a matter of no more than five minutes, the deluge ceases. The storm's cold front has passed over the island. And when I get home there are one or two stars to be seen through the breaking clouds. Tonight there will be squalls of hail and sleet; and, with that depression between here and Iceland moving steadily towards Scandinavia and pulling down north-westerlies from the Arctic, there will, within a day or so, be snow.

The roughness of Skye's weather and the harshness of its landscapes add, in some ways, to its appeal. In much of Britain, one of the world's most intensely cultivated and highly urbanised countries, there is no wild land left. In the island, in contrast, there is a good deal. And as more and more people set ever greater store by the opportunity to have access to such land, so political pressure mounts for measures designed to ensure that it remains inviolate.

Today, as a result, Skye is spattered with National Scenic Areas, Nature Reserves and Sites of Special Scientific Interest: all of them intended to preserve and protect particular pieces of territory; many of them bitterly resented by islanders to whom all such externally imposed designations are one more indication of the extent to which the resident population, now as in the past, is not permitted to have any worthwhile say in its own affairs.

The ensuing conflicts are inevitably aggravated by the fact that conservation organisations, both official and unofficial, are often represented in the Highlands and Islands by individuals who have no knowledge of, and little interest in, the people with whom they have to deal. Crofting communities — whose Gaelic culture, as already mentioned, is founded on a profound respect for nature and whose unintensive style of agriculture is primarily responsible for the survival of natural habitats of a type long since eradicated elsewhere in the British Isles — find themselves ordered about, as they see it, by English-accented scientists whose manner is, at best, condescending and, at worst, downright dictatorial.

Andrew Currie, the Nature Conservancy Council's man in Skye, is not like

Ruined cottages, Boreraig.

that. On the sort of December morning when a lowering mist fends off the dawn until after nine o'clock, he takes me to look at one of his woodland reserves, on the western side of Sleat, and tells me something about his own approach to conservation. You have to take your time, he says. You have to explain to people what you are about. And you have to show them that you understand their point of view.

'What worries me about the wider conservation movement,' Andrew remarks as we turn into Glen Meodal, 'is that it's so opposed to agriculture. There may be some justification for that in the south where modern farming methods have caused so much destruction. But there's no necessity for any such hostility in Skye. Here we have an ideal opportunity to develop ways of combining conservation, agriculture and forestry. And that's what we should be concentrating on; not wasting time on pointless rows with people who would be on our side if they were treated properly.'

A kilometre or so beyond Ord — where the road is not much more than a three-metre-wide strip of tarmac flung down on top of the hillside's unflattened contours — we stop and leave the car in one of the few spots in Skye where it is possible to park among naturally occurring trees. The road itself separates two types of woodland, Andrew explains. Towards the sea, almost invisible in the mist, the underlying rock is torridonian sandstone and on its acid soils there is no more than a scattering of oaks and birches. Above the road, however, is a limestone outcrop and on its more fertile soils there once flourished the ash forest which Andrew is now helping to restore.

The key to the woodland's regeneration is the two-metre-high fence which surrounds a substantial stand of trees, some of them more than 200 years old. Outside the fence, as is obvious from the closely browsed grass, both sheep and deer have free rein. Always hard pressed for food in winter, they nip out each seedling before it has a chance to mature; and by so doing they condemn the wood itself to eventual extinction. Inside the fence, on the other hand, the wood's lingering death has clearly been forestalled. All around are birch and ash saplings which are already, after only five or six years, approaching shoulder height.

With luck, Andrew says, his fence will remain stockproof for twenty years. At that point, a second section of woodland will be closed to the sheep and deer which will be allowed to return to the first section where an entire generation of trees will then be tall enough to withstand their grazing pressure. In this way the wood will be preserved and the sheep will benefit from increased shelter. It is, in Andrew's opinion, an example of how to serve both the nature conservation interest and the agricultural interest at the same time.

A fine rain is falling. It is oddly mild and windless for mid-winter; so calm that water droplets cling in long, quivering rows to the slender, purple coloured branches of the birch trees. 'In May,' Andrew remarks, 'this is my favourite part of Skye. The trees are just getting into leaf. The primroses are still in flower. And there's the sound of cuckoos. Take my advice and come back in spring. That's when you'll find Sleat at its best.'

Once much of the Highlands and Islands were more thickly wooded than

Salmon fishing station, Rigg, Trotternish.

the slopes above Ord are today. The red deer, now a lean and rangy beast of the open moor and hill, was then a forest animal, its numbers held in check by wolves. Eagles and buzzards ranged across great woods that stretched from the Atlantic to the North Sea and out of which the high peaks protruded like rocky islands in a dark green ocean. Bears rummaged among the trees. Wild boar churned up the underbrush. And northern Scotland's few human inhabitants went in awe of a natural world which they, unlike their more recent successors, were quite unable to dominate or control.

Then Skye and the West Highlands were indeed a wilderness. Now they are a wasteland; their bare, bleak hills and their unpeopled glens a consequence of human mismanagement, human greed and human nastiness. Nature can certainly flourish in the island, as it can flourish on a bomb site or on a motorway embankment. But to describe Skye as 'unspoiled', as is done frequently by southern conservationists and by those 'white settlers' mentioned earlier, is to abuse both language and history.

In the 1950s, before the conservation lobby was the force it is today, that point was made incisively by the Canadian novelist Hugh MacLennan, born in the Cape Breton mining town of Glace Bay and the great-grandson of a nineteenth-century emigrant from Kintail, on the Highland mainland opposite the island. In an essay entitled *Scotchman's Return*, MacLennan recorded his impressions of the place from which his ancestors had been expelled. And he grasped at once the essential difference between this manmade desolation and the true wilderness with which he was familiar in North America. Highland Scotland's wide open spaces, MacLennan conceded, bore a marked physical resemblance to those of the Canadian Arctic. 'But this Highland emptiness,' he continued, 'only a few hundred miles above the massed population of England, is a far different thing from the emptiness of our own North-west Territories. Above the 60th parallel in Canada you feel that nobody but God had ever been there before you. But in a deserted Highland glen you feel that everyone who ever mattered is dead and gone.'

That is a critical distinction. And it is impossible to be of Highland descent and not be aware of its importance. In another woodland nature reserve in another part of the West Highlands, I have stood on more than one occasion inside the crumbling and collapsing walls of the house that once belonged to my great-grandfather. My feelings then were the same as Hugh MacLennan's. And every one of the very many remnants of human habitation in the island has the capacity to engender similar emotions in someone; the cumulative effect of all such experiences being the negation of the notion that Skye is, or has been for more than a millenium, a wilderness in the strict sense of that much overused term.

The island has its share of wild country. It is replete with lonely places. Its landscape is both stark and grand. But the wild country, the lonely places and even the landscape itself are also, in far too many instances, the product of a prolonged process of environmental degradation, a good deal of it deliberate.

Most of Skye's once extensive woods were destroyed by man, exposing the newly denuded land to the leaching and weathering effects of wind and rain. The treeless moors and hills which resulted were then subjected to further erosion and deterioration through endemic overgrazing and burning. And to appreciate the extent of the ecological damage that has been done, one needs only to chart the stock-carrying capacity of a given tract of land over the 200 years since the introduction of extensive sheep farming. Where that capacity can be assessed accurately, it will be found to have fallen massively. And that fall has been paralleled, of course, by an equally drastic reduction in the human population.

That was the still neglected message of Frank Fraser Darling, the scientist and naturalist who did so much to ensure that conservation and ecology are among the dominant philosophical concepts of our time and whose early career was concerned almost exclusively with this north-western part of Scotland. 'And finally,' concludes the preface of one of Fraser Darling's numerous books about the region, 'the bald, unpalatable fact is emphasised that the Highlands and Islands are largely a devastated terrain and that any policy which ignores this fact cannot hope to achieve rehabilitation.'

The physical structure and climate of places like Skye, Fraser Darling insisted, is such that they 'are unable to withstand deforestation and maintain productiveness and fertility. Their history has been one of steadily accelerating deforestation until the great mass of the forests was gone, and thereafter of forms of land usage which prevented regeneration of tree growth and reduced the land to the crude values and expressions of its solid geological composition. In short, the Highlands are a devastated countryside and that is the plain primary reason why there are now few people and why there is a constant economic problem.'

Frank Fraser Darling's diagnosis, then, was far from hopeful. And his prognosis was profoundly pessimistic. 'Devastation has not quite reached its uttermost lengths,' he wrote in the 1950s, 'but it is quite certain that present trends in land use will lead to it and the country will then be rather less productive than Baffin Land.' It was possible, Fraser Darling agreed, that the abandoned and deserted nature of Highland landscapes would make them attractive to what he called 'the jaded townsman'. But any such appeal must necessarily be based on ignorance of the circumstances which had emptied the glens. 'If the jaded townsman attains to an ecological knowledge and appreciation,' Fraser Darling declared, 'he will not necessarily wish his wilderness to be the desolation caused through devastation of land by his own species. Man-made desolation is no environment for psychological health in a species as a whole.'

Today, unfortunately, the heirs of the environmentalist movement's founding father have jettisoned his broad perspective and made conservation, for the most part, the enemy rather than the ally of alterations in land use. Instead of seeking to heal the wounds which have been inflicted on the land, too many conservationists are content to preserve Skye's landscape as it now exists. And since the Royal Society for the Protection of Birds, to name just one of scores of conservation groups, has thirty or forty times more members

Mouth of the river Lealt with old salmon fishing station and diatomite works.

than there are people living on the island, this wholly negative approach may be the one which triumphs in the end.

And yet that need not be so; for there is surely present in the island, on the one hand, and in the wider conservation movement, on the other, the basis for a constructive alliance of the kind envisaged by Frank Fraser Darling for whom environmentalist thinking was the key to Highland progress. Such an alliance would be founded on an appreciation of the fact that the Skye landscape does not exist independently of the people who live on it. And its ultimate objective would be the adoption of management strategies which safeguard both the island's natural resources and the island's human population.

In devising such strategies, as Fraser Darling recognised, there can be no question of starting with a clean slate. This is not now the kind of country where only God has been before us. With the exception of the higher parts of the Cuillins and some of the more inaccessible coastal cliffs, no part of Skye is in its natural condition. Practically every corner of the island bears the marks of the ecologically extractive exploitation which began with the felling of the ancient woodlands and which ought now to be reversed: by planting more and more trees and by insisting that a high proportion of these trees are native species; by promoting the integration of forestry and agriculture; by increasing cattle numbers at the expense of sheep in order to improve the quality of much abused hill pastures; by assisting the local community to regain its long lost control of resource management.

The absence of localised decision-making is presently most keenly felt with regard to fisheries. Just as last century's landlords degraded the land in order to profit from sheep farming, so this century's fishing industry, by putting short-term gain ahead of long-term sustainability, has disastrously depleted fish stocks. And as has been amply demonstrated in Iceland and elsewhere, the one certain way to prevent such environmental calamities is to make fisheries management the responsibility of the one group with a vested interest in maintaining stocks at worthwhile levels: the people living beside the fishing grounds.

From Skye, from the Western Isles and from Shetland there have been repeated requests for the introduction of a fisheries management system designed to give priority to local boats; designed, too, to ensure that conservation measures are rigorously applied and that the financial benefits derived from island fisheries accrue primarily to islanders. But the external interests which dominate the fishing business are as powerful now as were those which previously wreaked so much ecological havoc ashore. And the days when herring and mackerel were plentiful in Skye sea lochs are, in consequence, long gone.

Undoing that type of damage and reasserting the primacy of island interests is necessarily difficult. The people who inhabit localities like Skye are a tiny minority in United Kingdom terms. If they are to improve their prospects politically, they need help. And one potential source of such assistance, or so it seems to me, are the many millions who now subscribe to the environmentalist ethic. A central component of that ethic is its stress on

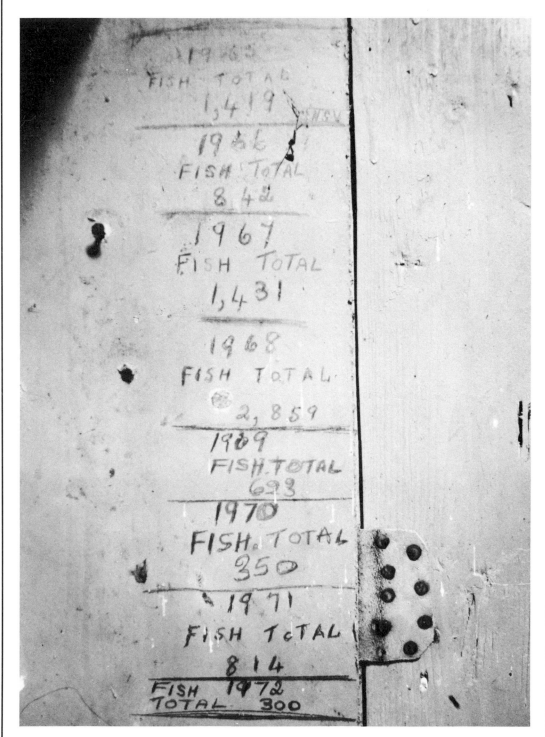

Yearly fish tally in Rigg salmon station.

the inherent desirability of maintaining smaller communities whose economies are based on renewable natural resources. And here in Skye there is no lack of opportunities to move in that direction.

A precondition of any such movement, however, is to free the available resources from the clutches of those who have mishandled them for so long and to restore the island's natural assets to island people. It is on that, I think, that conservationists ought to concentrate; not on erecting still more statutory barriers to changes in the present state of things. That way, after all, lies the demise of communities that sustain still a distinctive language and culture which are as precious, in their way, as the purely physical environment on which so much more emphasis is placed.

Were the Cuillins somehow defaced or disfigured by intrusive development, something precious would most certainly be lost. But should the Gaelic language be finally extinguished in its last Hebridean strongholds, then something else of value would be abstracted from the earth. And conservationists and ecologists, whose entire outlook is dominated by the need to maintain diversity of every kind, should surely be as concerned about the one as about the other. They should, in the manner of Frank Fraser Darling, who knew Skye well, be elaborating a vision of an island future in which community and culture are every bit as important as landscape, scenery and wildlife.

* * *

As we drive north again through Ferrindonald, Teangue and Isle Ornsay, the December sun breaks momentarily through the clouds and builds a rainbow right across the low Sleat hills. 'What annoys me most of all about the conservationist campaigners who come up here from the south,' says Andrew Currie, 'is their assumption that they appreciate Skye more than the people who actually live here. That's not my experience. Nobody's more aware than islanders themselves of just how beautiful this island really is.'

9

TO the west of the road between Bracadale and Dunvegan, in the north-western corner of the island, the view is dominated by those two, strangely flat-topped peaks, Healabhal Bheag and Healabhal Mor. Beyond them a ridge of lower hills runs roughly northwards, sheltering Loch Dunvegan from the prevailing westerly and south-westerly winds and ending abruptly in the sheer escarpment called Dunvegan Head. On the far side of this ridge — and, as a result, comparatively isolated from the rest of the island — is the long, shallow valley of Glendale.

On coming down into Glendale on the road from Dunvegan, you find that, at its northern end where it meets the fiord-like inlet of Loch Pooltiel, the glen widens into a crescent-shaped tract of reasonable land on which is situated a close-packed cluster of crofting townships. On the right bank of the Hamara River, which bisects the district, are Feriniquarrie, Glasphein and Fasach. Across the bridge which takes the road on towards Neist Point, Skye's westernmost extremity, are Holmisdale, Lephin, Hamara, Polosgan, Borrodale and Upper and Lower Milovaig.

In the last named of these small settlements, one hundred years ago, lived John MacPherson. He was in his late forties then; not tall, but nevertheless broad-shouldered; well-spoken in both Gaelic and English; heavily bearded in the manner of the time. He was, people said, a man of quite striking appearance. And because his speeches were printed in southern newspapers and his features reproduced in many of the illustrated magazines and journals of the period, he became, I suppose, the first Skye crofter to be both nationally recognised and nationally recognisable.

MacPherson was, by any reckoning, a rebel and a troublemaker. But there was good cause, he insisted, for the revolution which he did so much to start and to promote.

'We have very miserable dwelling-houses,' he said when asked, on one occasion, to describe the way in which he and his fellow crofters lived. 'They are thatched with straw; and as our crofts do not produce the required amount of straw necessary for fodder for cattle and thatch for our houses, and as we are prohibited from cutting rushes or pulling heather by the proprietor, the condition of our dwelling-houses in rainy weather is most deplorable. Above our beds comes down pattering the rain, rendered dirty and black by the soot on the ceiling above, through which, for want of thatch, the rain has free access.'

In preventing Glendale's crofters from gathering the rushes and heather which might have helped them waterproof their roofs, their landlord was displaying all the harsh and domineering vindictiveness that was characteristic of far too many men in his position. Indeed, at the beginning of January, 1882, in an apparently gratuitous attempt to reinforce their dictatorial regime, the local estate management issued a set of regulations designed to extend the already long list of banned activities. No crofter, it emerged, was to be allowed to keep a dog. And any driftwood washed up on the shore was henceforth to be considered the exclusive property of the Glendale estate. 'Notice is hereby given,' ran the proclamation pinned up on the local post-office as if it were, for all the world, an Act of Parliament, 'that the shepherds and herds on these lands have instructions to give up the names of any persons found hereafter carrying away timber from the shore that they may be dealt with according to law.'

In making such exorbitant claims, however, the estate authorities had finally overreached themselves. Within a day or two, their notice had been joined by another. And this one, though less immaculately penned, was to prove the more significant. 'We, the tenants of the estate of Glendale,' it announced, 'do hereby warn each other to meet at Glendale Church on the seventh day of February, at about one p.m., for the purpose of stating our respective grievances publicly.'

This was a daring move. And though the consequent gathering was not short of matters for debate, it became clear that the single most pressing complaint was what John MacPherson called 'want of land'. They would, the assembled crofters decided, ask the estate management to give them the tenancy of the nearby sheep farm of Waterstein — then out of lease — for which they were prepared to pay a reasonable rent. And well aware that they were running a considerable risk in even contemplating such a course, 'they one and all subscribed their names in a book', as was afterwards recalled, 'pledging themselves as a matter of honour to adhere in a body to the resolutions thus arrived at'.

The request for the tenancy of Waterstein was reduced to writing and sent to the Edinburgh lawyers who became the Glendale estate's trustees following the death of its cantankerous proprietor, Sir John Macpherson MacLeod. No response was forthcoming. But by the Glendale factor, Donald MacDonald, the crofters were at least assured, as John MacPherson recalled a year later, when these events had assumed national importance, 'that the trustees were coming to see us and that they would put matters right with us'.

What happened next, the Milovaig crofter was asked. 'The trustees did come in May,' he replied, 'and the weather was bad the night they came. But in

Crossing to Skye from Kyle of Lochalsh.

spite of that there was a bonfire on every hill. When they were a week in the place, we went to them. They gave us no satisfaction but told us to have patience. We told them that our forefathers had died in patience, that we ourselves had been waiting in patience till now and that we could not wait any longer.'

Some days after this confrontation came news of the trustees' verdict. The farm of Waterstein was to be let to their own factor, Donald MacDonald, a man who was already the tenant of two extensive holdings in other parts of Skye. This, as was recognised on all sides, amounted to a declaration of war. While the understandably nervous factor armed himself with a revolver, the Glendale crofters began a rent strike and drove their cattle and sheep on to the disputed land.

*   *   *

On a May morning, with the sun lighting up the green fields that slope down to Loch Mor, it is easy to see why the Milovaig crofters should have coveted Waterstein. 'My croft is about three acres of very shallow land,' John MacPherson said, 'and the other crofters in the townships of Upper and Lower Milovaig have the same amount of land and the same quality.' Such had been the case, he explained, since the 1840s when MacLeod of MacLeod, who then owned all this part of the island, had halved every one of the Milovaig crofts to make room for families whom he had evicted from their own homes in Bracadale. Before the number of holdings had been doubled in this way, John MacPherson went on, each Milovaig tenant had been able to keep six cows, sixteen sheep and a horse. Now no horses were carried on Lower Milovaig and, since their hill grazings had been reduced in proportion to their arable, none of the township's crofters could manage more than three cows and eight sheep. And yet here, within ten minutes walk of their cramped little village, was all this first-rate land!

First-rate or not, that land was soon to be a battlefield. Following the initial illegal incursion by the Milovaig tenants, the Glendale trustees obtained from no less a body than Scotland's Court of Session an interdict, or injunction, instructing the farm's invaders to remove their stock from Waterstein. John MacPherson and his neighbours, however, were not impressed by interdicts. Their sheep and cattle remained where they were all through the summer of 1882. And when, in November, two estate shepherds were sent to round up the offending beasts, they themselves were seized and mauled severely by a number of crofters.

Warrants were quickly issued for the arrest of the men responsible for the maltreatment of the shepherds. But the police, it transpired, did not dare enter the glen to put the warrants into effect. And as news of this extraordinary state of affairs began to percolate southwards, the national press began to interest itself in what was taking place in the island. 'In Glendale there are 500 men prepared for any emergency,' *The Times* reported breathlessly. 'They have committed a breach of interdict in forcibly possessing themselves of the Waterstein grazings and they have committed an assault on the landlord's shepherds. It is the opinion of the authorities that nothing short of a military force can possibly apprehend the offenders. The whole island of Skye is in a state of wild excitement.'

In Whitehall, too, Milovaig, Waterstein and other previously undreamed of places were under discussion by men more accustomed to partitioning Africa into handy-sized colonies than to dealing with unruly crofting townships. 'Profoundly as I regret the necessity for calling in military aid,' Scotland's premier law officer informed the home secretary, Sir William Harcourt, 'I do not see that the authorities have now any other course open to them.' From 10 Downing Street, however, the prime minister, William Gladstone, urged caution. The army was already bogged down in a frequently violent and certainly fruitless struggle with Irish smallholders and the premier had no wish to open a second front in Skye. Surely Inverness-shire's recently quadrupled police force could tackle the Milovaig crofters by themselves?

It was at the British cabinet's express insistence, therefore, that on January 16, 1883, an inspector, a sergeant and three constables set out from Dunvegan in an attempt to re-establish law and order in what the London newspapers now called the 'disaffected district' of Glendale.

A little to the north of the highest point on the road from Dunvegan to Glendale is a small hill called Ben Totaig. From its summit, this fine and springlike morning, I have an uninterrupted view eastward, across Eilean

Dubh, Eilean Mor, Gairbh Eilean and the quiet waters of Loch Dunvegan, to the village of Dunvegan itself — with, just a kilometre or so to the left, the squat, grey bulk of Dunvegan Castle outlined against the wooded policies on its inland side. Far away on my own left are the clearly visible hills of Harris. And by simply turning round, I can look down on Holmisdale and Milovaig where a few faint streamers of smoke can be seen above the irregular lines of sparkling-looking houses.

From vantage points like this, in the opening weeks of 1883, the Glendale men observed the only route into their valley. And when, that January day, they saw the advancing police detachment turn the corner at Colbost and set off up the brae towards them, the watchers were ready with a prearranged signal. At once, in the glen behind them, there was a hurried bustle of activity. As had no doubt happened centuries earlier, when a rival clan threatened or when potentially hostile galleys were glimpsed off Loch Pooltiel, horns were sounded and men mustered. And by the time the unfortunate inspector and his subordinates had drawn abreast of Ben Totaig and started down into Glendale, their mission was already doomed.

Their destination was Hamara Lodge. It is still there, abandoned now and with the hedges that once divided its walled garden run wild and turned into rows of straggling trees. Blackbirds are singing in these trees this morning. And the sun is reflected in the unwashed windows of upstairs rooms which, that January morning a century ago, were meant to assume the role of sleeping

Sheep fank.

quarters in a building which the authorities had decided to transform into a police barracks.

It was not to be. At the foot of the hill, between Fasach and Glasphein and with Hamara Lodge a couple of kilometres distant, the five policemen were met by a well-drilled crowd which the inspector later estimated to be some 500 strong. This 'mob', he reported to his superiors, consisted largely of young men, many of them 'armed with bludgeons'.

No words were exchanged. Instead the luckless officers were rushed, overwhelmed and knocked to the ground. They were then driven — 'like cattle', commented one witness — back across the hill to Colbost where, bruised and battered, they were left to retreat thankfully in the direction of Dunvegan.

Nor was this the end of the affair. Next day a court official from Edinburgh arrived in Glendale with a new batch of writs and interdicts which he hoped, a trifle optimistically, to serve on Waterstein's illegal occupiers. He, too, was firmly escorted off the estate. And then, on 20 January, a crowd calculated officially to number 1800 — though this, surely, was an exaggeration — gathered at Colbost with the aim, as soon became clear, of forcing the police to withdraw completely from the island's north-western quarter.

There was something of the appearance of a medieval peasants' revolt about that crowd. Its weapons were the common crofting implements of the time; hayforks, graips, sickles. Some men carried stout sticks. Others wielded crude pikes which had been made by lashing scythe blades to poles. Their mood was described as 'determined'. And the place on which they were marching, they said, was the Dunvegan hotel where the police had established a makeshift headquarters.

At the threatened hotel, meanwhile, an increasingly nervous police inspector was telegraphing Inverness for instructions. These, when they came, were unambiguous. Law and order would be restored some other day. For the moment, the men supposedly responsible for its maintenance were to retreat to the comparative safety of Portree.

That proved easier said than done, however. The police had no transport. And with something in the nature of an invading army about to descend on the village, Dunvegan's innkeepers and merchants refused point blank to provide the now thoroughly apprehensive inspector and his colleagues with as much as a horse and cart, let alone a carriage. In the face of this final setback, then, all pretence of a graceful withdrawal was abandoned. The advancing crofters, came new reports, had passed through Skinidin and were well on their way to Lonmore. Without waiting to hear any more, all the policemen present in Dunvegan simply took to their heels and set off across the hills in the direction of Edinbane.

*   *   *

Now even Mr Gladstone felt obliged to authorise government intervention. On the evening of 8 February, just as the cattle were being milked, a ship steamed slowly into Loch Pooltiel and dropped anchor in the

Old Cottage, Sligachan.

shelter of the little bay below Milovaig. In the gathering gloom her guns were difficult to distinguish. At her masthead, however, there could just be seen a white ensign. This, it was obvious, was a naval vessel; in fact, Her Majesty's gunboat *Jackal*. And comfortably installed in a cabin normally occupied by one of her officers was Malcolm MacNeil, the senior civil servant to whom the cabinet had entrusted the difficult job of opening negotiations with the Glendale crofters.

Because he was a close relative of several Highland landlords, and because he was consequently suspected of being predisposed to take the side of proprietor rather than tenant, MacNeil was not the ideal man to undertake the task of persuading the Milovaig people to abandon their rebellion. But he was one of the few men in government employment who spoke Gaelic. And that was felt, quite rightly, to be an essential qualification for what was bound to be a delicate mission.

MacNeil's orders were straightforward. He was to find out if the four men for whom warrants had been issued in connection with their part in the original attack on the Waterstein shepherds were prepared to give themselves up voluntarily. If the four, by far the most prominent of whom was none other than John MacPherson, were prepared to surrender in this way, then MacNeil was to have them put aboard the *Jackal* preparatory to their being brought to Edinburgh to stand trial. If the wanted men persisted in their defiance of the law, on the other hand, MacNeil was to make clear to them that troops would be sent to Glendale to secure their arrest.

On the morning following his gunboat's arrival in Loch Pooltiel, MacNeil came ashore and made his way to Glendale Free Church where he was to hold discussions with local crofters. The latter's spokesman, inevitably, was John MacPherson. 'He is 48 years of age,' wrote a journalist who watched the Milovaig crofter striding purposefully towards the church door, 'rather under the average size, of stout build and with a bushy whisker'. Asked by the same journalist to summarise the Glendale community's demands, MacPherson said bluntly: 'We want more land and there is plenty of it in the country.'

Once inside the church — where, exactly one year and two days before, the Glendale tenants had held the meeting at which they decided to apply for the Waterstein tenancy — MacPherson dominated the proceedings. In doing what they had done, he insisted, he and his fellow crofters were 'not going against the law of the country but against the law of the proprietors'. One of the four wanted men, Malcolm Matheson, was away from home, he added. But he and the two others, Donald MacLeod and John Morrison, were willing to stand trial — although, he added to roars of approval from the congested pews behind him, they were no more and no less guilty than every other person in Glendale.

On one thing, however, John MacPherson was adamant. No man, he declared, would leave Glendale a prisoner. Mr Matheson, Mr MacLeod and himself would certainly make their way to Edinburgh where they would equally certainly appear before the Court of Session. But they would go south as free men whose word alone would be a sufficient guarantee of their good conduct.

Glancing, no doubt, at the scribbling reporters at the back of the church and realising that John MacPherson had once again seized what a later generation would call the propaganda advantage, Malcolm MacNeil agreed to these conditions. On 12 February, to the ecstatic cheers of the dozens of wellwishers who had walked with them from their homes, the Glendale men boarded the *Dunara Castle* at Portree and began a journey that was to end in their being imprisoned for two months.

'Scotland is a land of peace and order,' they were told by the Lord President on being sentenced; and it was because they had so seriously and so flagrantly disturbed this peace and order that they were now being sent to jail. John MacPherson took a different view. 'I got sixty-one days in prison for telling the truth and asking for justice,' he said. But as he settled down in his cell in Edinburgh's Calton Jail with the Gaelic Bible which he had requested from the prison's governor, the man from Milovaig knew he had helped secure more than the title of 'Glendale martyr' which the press had already bestowed on him.

As the *Jackal* rounded Neist Point and steamed back towards her base on the Clyde, Malcolm MacNeil had begun composing his considered report on the Glendale episode. It was of vital importance, he urged, that the government should initiate its own objective investigation into the causes of the troubles in Skye. And on 26 February, 1883, a fortnight before the Glendale men were

Sunset from Elgol.

jailed, the House of Commons were duly informed that the cabinet proposed to make crofting grievances the subject of a royal commission of inquiry.

Turning left at Colbost, where there are new leaves on the hazel bushes and new lambs in the fields, I make for Husabost on the western shore of Loch Dunvegan. Here, as the township's crofters told Mr Gladstone's grudgingly granted royal commission when its members visited the district in May 1883, there survived longer than anywhere else in the British Isles the essentially medieval and feudal practice whereby a landlord was permitted to exact unpaid work from his tenants.

'Ten days work was claimed by the proprietor from each crofter at spring and harvest labour,' explained Magnus MacLean, a Husabost tenant. That work had to be performed at times when crofters were busiest on their own holdings, he went on. And it had to be done with tools and implements which people were forced to buy for the purpose. There was no escape; there were no exemptions. If a particular tenant was absent when his presence was required by the laird, his wife had to turn out in his place. Should neither husband nor wife be able to put in an appearance, for whatever reason, a fine would be levied by the estate management. And if that fine were not paid promptly, then the offender would be threatened with eviction.

His own case, Magnus MacLean continued, was typical of the rest. He remembered coming home, on one occasion, from the east coast herring fishing which he attended annually. It was harvest time and his wife had been ordered to assist with the reaping of the landlord's corn. However, news was brought to her of her husband's return and, since he had been four months away, she naturally wished to see him. 'She asked as a favour of the factor to be allowed to go home,' Magnus MacLean said bitterly, 'and she would not get leave.'

John MacPherson was to help to change all that. Released from prison in the month that the royal commission came to Skye, he threw himself into the task of getting crofters everywhere to band together in a concerted campaign for improved conditions. The political organisation that emerged as a result was called the Highland Land League and the Milovaig crofter was one of its most effective and enthusiastic advocates. 'It would be as easy to stop the Atlantic Ocean,' he said, 'as to stop the present agitation until justice has been done to the people.' And he was right. Faced with mounting disorder in Skye and faced with a small but vociferous phalanx of Highland Land League MPs in the Commons, the government passed, in 1886, an Act which gave crofters everywhere security of tenure. No longer could their landlords remove island people from their homes and holdings. There would be no more clearances.

At the point where the Glendale road enters Dunvegan is a large and graceless building. It is a factory where a locally based firm manufactures sophisticated electronic equipment. This is not the sort of enterprise which most visitors to the island expect to discover here. But its existence, I think, would have pleased John MacPherson. He was altogether in favour of economic development of every kind and, like me, he saw nothing at all attractive about either black houses or backwardness.

10

ABOUT five kilometres beyond Dunvegan, on the way to Portree, is the stone archway called Fairy Bridge. Once it carried the main road. Now it has been bypassed and stands unused, fenced-off and isolated at the foot of heather-covered slopes which have something of the hollowed out shape of an amphitheatre. Here, in the 1840s, at Beul-Atha-Nan-Tri-Allt, the confluence of the three burns, huge crowds gathered weekly to sing psalms, to pray and to listen to the sermons of Roderick MacLeod, *Maighstir Ruari*, the one Skye minister who denounced the clearances and identified wholeheartedly with the cause of the common people.

A good deal of the intense religious feeling that is still to be detected in Skye had its origins in these emotional conventicles at Fairy Bridge. And though some southerners have long made mock of the island variant of Christianity, and of its sabbatarian tendencies in particular, there has always seemed to me to be something indisputably noble about the faith of the men and women who came here to look, quite simply, for the hope and comfort which were so lacking in their everyday lives.

The influence of the Church on island people continues to be much debated. And as well as those who find that influence amusing, there are those who think it pernicious; believing organised religion in the various more or less stringent manifestations which it has adopted in Skye, to have suppressed or even destroyed all that was best in the island's traditional Gaelic culture.

That the Church was no friend of many aspects of that culture is quite obvious. *Maighstir Ruari* himself denounced dancing and singing and shinty and much else. But to imply, in consequence, that he and his disciplines somehow imposed a wholly negative and alien creed on Skye's population is to insult, I think, the memory of the people who met here at Beul-Atha-Nan-Tri-Allt. They came willingly to Fairy Bridge these people, tramping all the way from Glendale and Bracadale, Dunvegan, Edinbane and Waternish. And it was from among their own ranks, after all, that there had first emerged the beliefs which Roderick MacLeod so capably articulated.

Binn na Caillich from Lochain Dubha.

Hayfield, Trumpan, Waternish.

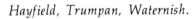

Snowstorm on the Sound of Raasay.

The nineteenth-century ecclesiastical establishment had little to offer the folk of Suisnish, Meadale and Sumardale. Their Church of Scotland ministers were appointed and installed by the lairds responsible for the ruining of such communities. And these same ministers, very often, attributed all such calamities to Skye people's own inherent wickedness. The landlord who ordered an eviction, it was suggested, was merely the instrument of God's wrath and was not to be blamed for his actions. Not the laird, but his victims, had sinned. And they were suffering in consequence.

These desperately dreary doctrines served to keep Skye's parish ministers firmly in the affections of the landed proprietors who were their paymasters. But they also emptied island churches and opened the way for alternative modes of worship. Soon there had emerged, in place of the discredited clerics, local lay preachers like Donald Munro, a blind man who, on being converted to a fiercely evangelical and fundamentalist brand of Christianity, put away the fiddle of which he had been an acknowledged master, and set about the task of spreading his novel creed throughout the island. 'No gentleman,' it was observed, 'associated with Donald Munro'; for his was a religion of the commonalty. And however hostile it may have been to secular song and poetry, it was equally hostile to the landowners whose policies posed such an evident threat not just to Gaelic tradition but to Gaeldom itself.

Men of Munro's stamp, and there were many of them, had little in the way of formal education. Nor did their backgrounds differ markedly from those of the people to whom they preached in island homes and on island hillsides. Roderick MacLeod, in contrast, was of aristocratic descent. And he was already an ordained minister of the Church of Scotland when he was suddenly persuaded of the spiritual virtues of the revivalist movement then gathering momentum all about him. In thus abandoning his previous convictions, Roderick MacLeod chose to isolate himself from his clerical colleagues who, accordingly, condemned him as a rabble-rouser and a traitor to his class. But he also became the acknowledged leader of the faith then developing outside the institutional church.

Maighstir Ruari was a singularly impressive man. He had, said one admirer, 'the head of an Apollo and the soul of a saint'. As a Gaelic preacher he was quite outstanding. And as a scourge of island landowners he was then unmatched. One visitor to Skye found him to be 'an enemy of emigration'; something that was in itself remarkable at a time when all established opinion favoured a deliberately depopulating policy. 'He considers the earth ought to be cleared of sheep and not of men,' runs a surviving account of a conversation with Roderick MacLeod, 'and he affirms that the island is capable of maintaining every soul upon it; but under different government.'

There was to be no 'different government' in Skye in Roderick MacLeod's time. There was, however, to be a different Church. In 1843 the Church of Scotland lost a third of its total following to a breakaway group who proclaimed that church members, and not the landed gentry, should select a congregation's minister. The dissident faction entitled themselves, provocatively, the Free Church. And *Maighstir Ruari* immediately led almost all

The Bile, north of Portree.

of Skye's adult population into the new denomination.

Because the Free Church had so much popular backing, and because it was founded on an explicitly anti-landlord principle, its adherents were openly persecuted by island proprietors. Donald Matheson, a Portree man who took a prominent part in raising funds for the Free Church, was promptly evicted by Lord Macdonald who also refused to allow the then propertyless organisation to build churches in any of the seven parishes which he owned.

And so Roderick MacLeod took to the moors and hills in the manner of Donald Munro. On Sunday after Sunday he preached to the thousands who came from practically every part of the island to the little glen at Fairy Bridge. Often it rained. Sometimes it was stormy. But neither the elements nor Lord Macdonald were to be permitted to stand in the way of the Free Church. On one occasion, Roderick MacLeod recalled, he was holding a service on the open slopes above Uig when it began to snow. Within a few minutes, he said, he could 'hardly distinguish' his congregation from the ground on which they sat or squatted. But *Maighstir Ruari*'s listeners, it seems, made no attempt to leave. Such a thing would just not have occurred to them.

*   *   *

John MacPherson, too, came frequently to Beul-Atha-Nan-Tri-Allt; for it was here, in a deliberate evocation of the earlier battle for religious freedom, that the Highland Land League staged the monster meetings at which Skye

River Sligachan.

Strathaird.

Ben Tianavaig from the Creag Mhor.

people affirmed their claims to the crofts on which they lived and the farms from which they had been removed.

These meetings, like the gatherings called by *Maighstir Ruari*, began and ended with psalm and prayer. And the impassioned oratory to be heard at them was generously interspersed with scriptural allusion and quotation; for it was to his Gaelic Bible that a crofter turned instinctively for proof that the land was his and not his landlord's. 'The earth He hath given to the children of men,' declared Donald MacCallum, the Waternish minister jailed for his Land League involvement. 'The land is our birthright, even as the air, the light of the sun and the water belong to us as our birthright.'

In the crowd at Fairy Bridge, on that occasion, was Mary MacPherson, *Mairi Mhor nan Oran*, big Mary of the songs, whose compositions best reflect the spirit of the Land League uprising. 'We saw the breaking of the horizon and the clouds of slavery dispelled,' she believed, 'on the day that MacCallum stood with us at Beul-Atha-Nan-Tri-Allt.' And for a moment, just a moment, there was nothing that seemed impossible. There would be no more landlords. There would be no tyranny. The Gaels would repossess the places from which they had been expelled. 'And when I am in my coffin,' *Mairi Mhor* foretold, 'my words will be as a prophecy; and there will return the stock of the tenantry who were driven over the sea. And the gentry will be routed as they, the crofters, were. Deer and sheep will be wheeled away and the glens will be tilled; and the cold, ruined stances of houses will be built on by our kinsmen.'

* * *

Today at Fairy Bridge, there is little sign that Mary MacPherson's vision will ever be made a reality. There is no shouting, no cheering; there are no demands now to turn the world upside down. From the moors below Ben Horneval and Beinne na Boineide there comes only the distant bleating of the sheep that *Mairi Mhor* so detested. And yet she was right, I think, to insist that the island need not be poor, half empty and futureless. Skye was not in her day, and is not in our's, a place without resources. It is the way that these resources have been managed — or mismanaged — which has deprived island people of the chance to reshape their surroundings and their circumstances in the way advocated by Mary of the Songs.

Skye's problems, in the nineteenth century at any rate, were not the outcome of any absolute absence of wealth. Immense fortunes were made from kelp. Sheep farming, in its heyday, generated massive revenues. The trouble was that all except a miniscule minority of the island's population were rigorously excluded from the resulting bonanza. Skye people's annual output of kelp was worth many millions of pounds at today's prices. But their landlords were the sole beneficiaries and, to make matters worse, island lairds were not greatly interested in investing their considerable capital in any very productive fashion.

'The solid advantages which the new tide in their affairs had opened up to them,' wrote the Victorian journalist Robert Somers of Skye proprietors' response to the kelp boom, 'were bartered for the merest baubles.' To be seen to live grandly was of much more importance than to attend to the island's long-term needs. Thus Lord Macdonald spent a good deal of his kelp-inflated income on his new mansion at Armadale. The building, as eventually constructed, was a lot less lavish than its noble incumbent had hoped it would be. The collapse in kelp prices saw to that. Even so, a single window in Armadale Castle, as Somers commented forcefully, was said to have cost more than a hundred of Lord Macdonald's kelping tenants would have earned in a year. Such was the utterly inequitable end product of the various transformations which Skye's landowners and their apologists liked to call 'improvements'.

The island's fate in the imperial era, then, was not dissimilar to that of much of the Third World. Just as the West African peasant was forced to supply the British market with cocoa beans which enriched their exporters, their importers and the chocolate manufacturing companies, so the Skye crofter was obliged to provide the kelp which made both island lairds and southern industrialists wealthy men. Neither the West African smallholder nor his Skye counterpart, however, benefited in any way from their involuntary involvement in this type of economic development. Often they were worse off when it ended than they had been before it began; having been impoverished by being made to sell their raw materials at knock-down prices; and having been debarred from processing and refining these materials for their own financial betterment.

Shed made from upturned boat.

Beinn Dearg.

Aird Bhearnasdail.

Beinn a' Chearcaill.

All such processing adds greatly to the value of the commodities affected by it. A litre of petrol costs a lot more than a litre of crude oil. A knitted garment is worth much more than the wool which went into it. A neatly packaged fish fillet in a supermarket freezer is an altogether costlier item than a freshly landed haddock on the pier.

The localities where such processing takes place are also richer than those which supply the original raw materials. The country which makes car tyres is wealthier than the one which merely provides rubber. The city with a chocolate factory is better off than the community which grows cocoa beans. The nation that manufactures steel is wealthier than the one which relies on exporting iron ore. And the explanation for these disparities is straightforward: the region which confines its economic role to the supply of raw materials deprives itself of the revenues and employment generated by the processing operations which its raw materials make possible.

No community, of course, enters freely or eagerly into such a subordinate relationship with others. It does so because it has no alternative; as a consequence, in the past, of having been incorporated forcibly into a colonial empire; as a consequence, in more modern times, of being unable to alter the discriminatory and coercive financial and other arrangements which outside agencies apply to it. To break out of debilitating dependence of this type, then, is not easy. Despite their political independence, many former colonies in Africa and Asia have not yet managed to do so. Nor have Skye and other parts of the West Highlands.

Its land, which remains the island's basic resource, is not owned by the communities which live upon it. The fish which are still to be taken in island waters are not generally caught by island boats and are usually processed in distant centres. The salmon farms which are common now in Skye sea lochs are the property, very often, of multinational companies. The forests which are being planted on island hills seldom belong to islanders. In almost every instance, in short, the profits from these widely varying activities, all of them dependent on the exploitation of island resources, will be of no more benefit to island people than were the profits made from the kelp business of almost two centuries ago.

Forestry is characteristic of what has gone so sadly wrong; for the extensive plantations to be seen in Skye and the rest of the Scottish Highlands are owned either by the Forestry Commission, a state agency, or by externally based private corporations which are run in the interests of the faraway financiers who invest in them. A modicum of low paid employment is provided in these forests. But there is no worthwhile local participation in the ownership and management of a resource which is clearly one of immense potential in a world which is running out of wood and in a country which has long had to import more than ninety per cent of its timber requirements.

Our failure to enable Highland and Island communities to benefit directly from the plantations springing up around them is all the more extraordinary in view of the contrasting experience of comparable countries overseas. On the island, as in all of northern Scotland, crofting and forestry are organised in

Trotternish from Raasay with Raasay House in foreground.

such a way as to have practically nothing to do with one another. In much of continental Europe, where these things are handled much more sensibly, farmers and smallholders are able to profit from their own patch of woodland, which they generally manage very well, in exactly the same way as they benefit from their crops and stock. In Switzerland, for example, two thirds of the nation's forests are owned by the people who live beside them and among them. Local ownership is also common in Germany, France and Belgium. And in Sweden and Finland nearly a quarter of all forestry is closely integrated with agriculture at the level of the family farm.

Unlike the larger and more remote concerns which dominate forestry in Scotland, the farmer who is also a forester has an intimate knowledge of local conditions. He can modify planting patterns to take account of these conditions. He can apply more intensive and more careful management techniques to his trees. He can ensure that his forestry operations boost his agricultural output: by making the best possible use of shelter belts and by employing woodland grazing systems. The farmer-forester can supply his own fenceposts, building materials and firewood. He can provide himself and his family with useful employment at otherwise slack times of year. Above all, he can counter the otherwise inevitable tendency for forestry revenues to be appropriated by some essentially extraneous combine consisting primarily of businessmen whose interests are such as to make it extremely unlikely that these revenues will ever be invested in ways that assist the inhabitants of

The Trotternish Hills.

Crofts, Digg.

River Sligachan with An Leitir in the background.

those localities where the trees are actually grown.

All this we could achieve in Skye, as it has already been achieved in Scandinavia and the Alpine countries, if we were prepared to challenge the many people now doing as well at our expense as last century's landlords did at the expense of our predecessors. Of course, it will not be easy to bring about the political and other changes needed to ensure that island crofters and hill farmers become the major beneficiaries of continuing afforestation. Nor will it be a simple matter to introduce fisheries management methods which give priority to island fishermen. Nor, indeed, will there be any shortage of obstacles in the way of breaking the hold which powerful financial interests now exert over the rapidly expanding fish farming industry. But that does not imply that the necessary effort should not be made. Only by such means, after all, will island people ever be able to take full advantage of island resources. And only by such means will Skye be made the place which Mary MacPherson believed it ought to be. That her prophecy has so far failed of fulfilment, as Sorley MacLean once observed, is not the fault of the big, brave heart of *Mairi Mhor nan Oran*. It is the fault of those of us who have come after her.

* * *

At the head of Loch Greshornish, just below Edinbane, a heron is standing stiffly and patiently in the shallows. Nobody tries to stop these big, grey birds, which are common on Skye, from fishing where they like. Should you try to follow their example, however, you may find yourself in trouble. The island's landlords believe they own the salmon in its rivers and the deer on its hills; and the law is very firmly on their side. Steal someone's purse while strolling though Portree and you will probably be fined. Take a fish from a hill burn and you could go to jail.

That does not stop people poaching, though. I have done it myself; slipping along a river's edge at dusk and searching out a salmon with the help of a carefully shielded torch. Having found a fish at rest below the bank, you step back a little and fasten to the end of your walking stick — with a piece of stout twine carried for that purpose — an ordinary rabbit snare. Leaning out over the water, you guide the snare carefully over the salmon's gently moving tail. And then you pull. Within a second or so, the now helpless fish is on the grass beside you.

The motive for such ploys is partly practical. A sizeable salmon, boiled and eaten cold, will provide a family with two or three good dinners. But there is also the sheer joy of having defied the landowner and the law; the pleasure of having asserted, once again, those claims which, irrespective of the judgments of the courts and pronouncements of parliamentarians, all islanders refuse stubbornly to relinquish. 'It is not easy to convince a Highlander that a landlord has a better right to a deer, a moorfowl or a salmon than he has himself,' wrote one despairing friend of northern Scotland's proprietors as long ago as 1802, 'because he considers them the unconfined bounty of heaven.'

The Highland tradition had no place for the peculiar notion that one or two wealthy individuals should be able to establish an exclusive claim to the products of nature. As one well-known Gaelic proverb has it, everyone is entitled to a deer from the mountain, a tree from the wood and a fish from the river. And there has never seemed, to the ordinary Highlander, to be either logic or morality in the landowning lobby's continuing attempts to have it otherwise. 'The fish that was yesterday miles from land was claimed by the landlord the moment it reached the shore,' declared a Skye crofter at a Highland Land League meeting in 1884. 'And so also were the birds of the air as soon as they flew over his land. The law made it so because the landlords themselves were the lawmakers; and it was a wonder that the poor man was allowed to breathe the air of heaven and drink from the mountain stream without having the factor and the whole of the county police pursuing him as a thief.'

And what was thought by the people to be true of the wild animals on the land was thought to be true, too, of the land itself. The ground on which they lived, the ground on which they grew their crops and reared their goats and cattle, was not, to the islanders of several centuries ago, an ordinary commodity that could, or should, be bought and sold for cash as if it were no different from a peddler's trinkets. It was not that they believed the land belonged to those who worked it. The entire concept of private property in land would have made no more sense to them than the idea that a man might own the clouds or take out a financial interest in the ocean. The land, it was

The Red Cuillin from Raasay.

Healaval Mor, one of 'MacLeod's Tables'.

Tarskavaig, Sleat.

Tarskavaig, Sleat.

assumed, had been made by God for humanity's benefit; and one person's claim to its use was as good as that made by another.

'The earth He has given to the children of men,' explains the Old Testament which every nineteenth-century crofter knew as few other people have known it. And it was on texts like this that the Skye leaders of the Land League took their stand. 'Unless landlords can prove that we are not of Adam's race at all,' observed John MacPherson in a letter which he sent to MacLeod of MacLeod, at Dunvegan Castle, in November 1884, they could not demonstrate that their entitlement to the land was in any way superior to that of their crofting tenants. In more than one place in scripture, MacPherson continued, were 'letters of agreement from God pronouncing our claim and right in the land'. And who was MacLeod of MacLeod to argue with that?

'If the landlords consulted Moses or Joshua,' said Norman Stewart from Valtos, making the same point at a mass meeting in Kilmuir in 1885, 'they would find there substantial evidence as to who are the rightful owners of the soil.' The government's representatives were in the habit of citing legal precedent and parliamentary statute, Stewart went on. But crofters could turn to an infinitely higher authority than these. 'Sheriff Ivory can quote Acts George and John,' declared Norman Stewart. 'But we can quote the Act of God, the Bible.'

* * *

The Macdonald estates, which once accounted for the greater part of Skye were sold off, bit by bit, until, in the 1970s, they disappeared completely. And successive MacLeods of MacLeod have presided over a similar, though not yet quite so drastic, disposal of their inheritance. That has left the state, in the shape of the Department of Agriculture and the Forestry Commission, as the island's most substantial proprietor. But the land which has thus been nationalised is no more controlled by the people who live on it than is the land which remains in private hands. And of the latter there is a good deal. For while Skye's modern lairds, with the exception of MacLeod of MacLeod, are not the heirs of the men who organised the clearances, the individual landlord still looms large. And on the concerns, the character and the whims of such a person, much — too much, in my opinion — can depend.

Among the island's lairds are men who have a genuine interest in developing their estates in such a way as to enhance local employment prospects. But the fact that their properties are better run than many others does not seem to me to make private landownership any more attractive as an institution; just as the fact, for instance, that India was, on the whole, well governed by its British rulers does not justify the existence of colonialism.

The island has always had good landlords as well as bad. One MacLeod laird made considerable financial sacrifices in order to feed his tenants at a time of hunger. Another MacLeod laird cleared most of Minginish and Bracadale. And against the generally admirable record of some of today's proprietors there may be set the contrary experience of Waternish, the locality to the north of Fairy Bridge. Here, in the 1970s, a landlord who was a folksinger was

Sun on wet rocks in the Cuillin.

Struan Post Office.

Bagpipes laid out at the Skye Games.

Morning mist, Skeasbost from Bernisdale.

Treaslane River in spate.

succeeded by a landlord who was a businessman of sorts in Holland. And so complex were the ensuing sales, purchases, transfers and speculations that, in the end, nobody — not the local authority, not the relevant government agencies and certainly not the families living there — had any idea as to whom a substantial slice of Waternish belonged.

That one landlord is better or worse than another is neither here nor there. Last century's evictions did not happen because this particular Lord Macdonald or that particular MacLeod of MacLeod was a peculiarly nasty piece of work. Rather the clearances were the inevitable outcome of a landholding system which made it incumbent upon the proprietor to maximise his income without having any necessary regard for the interest of the rest of the community. It is not in any way accidental that in comparable parts of Europe where there were no huge estates and where a smallholding population retained its own stake in the land, there was not, in the nineteenth century, the terrible poverty that was so prevalent in Skye. Nor did there occur in such places, and Norway is a prime example, violent dispossessions and expulsions of the type which were so common in the island and the rest of north-west Scotland.

Because the land on which they lived did not belong to them, Skye's nineteenth-century inhabitants were denied the opportunity to manage that land in such a way as to enable all the island's people to benefit from its development. Skye's twentieth-century population is similarly deprived. Both private landownership and state landownership, however well intentioned, have the effect of making it impossible for island communities to be responsible for their own future. And until such responsibility is granted to them, by enabling each island locality to take sole charge of its land and its natural resources, Skye people will never be in full command of their own lives.

11

THE Free Church which emerged in the 1840s survives still in the island. In Scotland as a whole its membership was reduced massively some 50 years ago as a result of the majority of its worshippers rejoining the Church of Scotland. In the Highlands and Islands, however, the Free Church retains a good deal of the popular support it first won in the nineteenth century — although in Skye, as in some other places, it has had to cope with more than one split in its own ranks. These schisms have resulted, as far as the island is concerned, in the Free Church and the Church of Scotland now having to distinguish themselves doctrinally from the Free Presbyterian Church as well as from each other. And maintaining the necessary distinctions is made all the more complicated by the fact that both the Free Church and the Free Presbyterians consider themselves heir to the particular brand of spirituality associated with the likes of *Maighstir Ruairi*. But whatever their differences, neither of the two smaller denominations think very highly of the modern Church of Scotland which they believe, with some justification, to set more store by wishy-washy moralising and socially conscious politicking than by the intellectually rigorous theology that was long the hallmark of the Scottish brand of protestantism.

At Uig, in the northern part of the island, the Free Church place of worship stands on a prominent knoll on the southern outskirts of the village. It is, like most island kirks, severely functional. Its exterior is angular in shape and grey in colour. And at its north-western corner is a square-built tower which, as if in recognition of the once common supposition that such features betray an episcopal or even catholic orientation, has been denied the elevation needed to transform it into a steeple. Outside a noticeboard announces, in faded gold lettering, that sabbath services take place at 12.00 noon, in English, and at 6.00 p.m., in Gaelic. Sabbath school is at 3.15 p.m. And there is a weekly prayer meeting on Thursday evenings. All are welcome.

Uig, as viewed from its Free Church building, is placid enough. There is a steady humming of generators from the Western Isles ferry moored at the end

Boundaries at Toravaig.

Ard Mor, Waternish.

Ben Tianavaig from Toravaig.

of the south-eastward jutting pier which practically encloses the bay's northern quarter. A fishing boat, making for the sheltered anchorage which the pier provides, is churning slowly into the bay with the usual quota of gulls hovering expectantly over its wake. Beyond Waternish Point and the Ascrib Islands, their low shapes dark against a sea which seems smooth and polished in the afternoon light, it is raining. But here the sun is shining on the crofts at Idrigill above the ferry terminal and there is not enough wind to move the branches of the trees at the foot of the brae below the church.

Down there, on a narrow strip of comparatively flat ground between sea and hill, are Scots pine, beech and ash of a larger size than is normal in Skye. The resulting stand of timber, although obviously neglected nowadays, has the appearance generally associated with the wooded policies which last century's lairds were in the habit of establishing in the vicinity of their homes. All that is missing, in this case, is the mansion, or 'big house', itself. It was destroyed one day in 1877. And its destruction, as it may be appropriate to recall in the grounds of the local Free Church, was widely believed hereabouts to amount to a divine judgment on its owner. His name was William Fraser and, a number of years before the 1877 disaster, he had bought the Kilmuir estate, as his property was known, from a financially embarrassed Lord Macdonald.

Fraser's lands, occupying the bulk of the peninsula which extends due north from Portree, were among the most desirable in Skye. And they are still agriculturally productive. From Uig northward through Totescore, Linicro, Balgown, Kilmuir itself, Hungladder, Osmigarry and Duntulm to Kilmaluag, near the island's northern extremity, are to be found many well stocked and well managed crofts. And though the townships on the peninsula's eastern flank, from Flodigarry down through Staffin to Elishader, Valtos, Culnaknock, Lonfearn and Lealt, are on rather less fertile soils, they, too, are mostly active crofting communities.

Fraser inherited a number of sheep farms from his Macdonald predecessors. But that did not stop him organising the island's last clearance in order to put still more land under sheep. Nor did the fact that much of the best land in the locality had previously been transferred forcibly from crofters to farmers prevent the Kilmuir estate's proprietor increasing croft rents to levels far above those prevailing elsewhere on the island.

'Our principal grievance,' said Malcolm Nicolson from Sheader near Uig, 'consists of our rents having been raised three times.' His own annual rent, he explained, had practically doubled and stood at more than £12.00 — a sum which a labourer would then have taken several months to earn. Others had suffered even greater exactions. But the Sheader tenants had been especially ill used, Malcolm Nicolson remarked forcefully, because higher rents were being levied, in their case, on demonstrably inferior holdings. 'Our original crofts were turned into a sheep farm beside us,' he said. 'We were all removed. It was Major Fraser who removed us.'

'Having purchased his estate under the laws of the country,' William Fraser responded, 'he had a perfect right to lay it out and improve it as he thought fit.'

Gable end, Bearraraig Bay.

Many people did not approve of that, of course. Many people were far too prone to attribute all their misfortunes to lack of land and to imagine that all their difficulties would be at an end if their crofts were enlarged. In truth, said the Kilmuir laird, the 'crofting system' itself was 'the cause of most of the poverty in Skye'. And the 'best remedy', in his opinion, would be 'a certain amount of emigration properly arranged to suitable countries'.

Although he claimed to have a 'personal liking' for his tenantry, Fraser's views were such as to make clear that he had as little respect for their aspirations as they had for his. And in this mutual antipathy is to be found the origin of the recriminations which were to follow the deluge that descended on the Kilmuir estate on October 13, 1877.

* * *

The year had already produced some extraordinarily bad weather. In January and February almost all of northern Scotland had been snow-covered for several weeks. Blizzards had been frequent. Railway transport had been seriously disrupted. And though March and April had brought some

The Storr from Sartle.

Staffin from the Quirang.

improvement, there had been little in the way of spring. May, too, was unusually cold. And the summer was equally unfavourable, turning out wet, cool and stormy.

October 1877 began in the manner of immediately preceding months. On 10 October, Skye experienced severe gales which were accompanied by snow, thunder and lightning; 11 October was also wild and windy. Next day there was serious flooding in the southern part of the island. And on 13 October, with the wind now in the south-west, quite exceptional daily rainfall totals were recorded at various points in Skye and the West Highlands.

In Dunvegan there were four-and-a-half inches of rain that day. In Portree there were five inches. And had there been a rain gauge in the vicinity of Uig, it has been estimated, it would have measured more than seven inches. For it was in the Uig area, on the estate belonging to the detested William Fraser, that the storm and its associated cloudburst were at their most intense.

The river which flows through these thickly wooded policies below Uig's Free Church is called the Conon. And on 13 October, 1877, it was transformed into a raging torrent. Brown, muddy, filled with uprooted trees and other debris, it roared into Uig Bay until, a kilometre or so up Glen Uig, at a spot not far from Malcolm Nicolson's croft at Sheader, its course was suddenly blocked by a landslide. The earth dam that resulted was soon breached. A wall of water hurtled down the narrow, rocky gorge which connects Glen Uig with the sea. Boulders weighing as much as one or two tons were rolled along in the spate.

Wind on Loch Fada.

Uig's ancient burial ground was inundated. And so was Uig Lodge, the Skye residence of Major William Fraser of Kilmuir.

Because the lodge was downstream from the already overwhelmed graveyard, the chaos which ensued was of a particularly grisly character. Coffins which had been broken open by the flood lay among the mud and silt in Fraser's garden. Here and there were skulls, skeletons and little piles of human bones. The corpse of one of the laird's most recently evicted tenants, it was rumoured, had actually been discovered in the ruins of the major's living room.

There matters may have rested but for the fact that an account of the flood and its consequences was sent to an Inverness newspaper, *The Highlander*, whose editor, John Murdoch, was then emerging as a persistent, unbending and extremely effective critic of Highland landlords. The paragraphs forwarded from Skye that October were clearly designed to conform with the paper's radical line. Unfortunately, they were also libellous.

The offending story, headed *The Uig Disaster*, began innocuously enough. 'The havoc done on the Kilmuir estate,' it ran, 'is beyond description.' But having dealt briefly with broken bridges, damaged roads and other calamities, Murdoch's contributor warmed to his theme. And his theme, it emerged, was only indirectly related to the effects of the island's atrocious weather. 'The belief throughout the parish,' it was claimed, 'is that the disaster is a judgment upon Major Fraser's property. It is very remarkable, it is said, that all the destruction of property on Skye is confined to his estate. Again it is strange that nearly all the dead buried in Uig during the last 500 years should be brought up as it were against his house, as if the dead in their graves arose to perform the work of vengeance which the living had not the spirit to execute.'

This was strong stuff. And if John Murdoch, a very wily journalist, had been on hand to check his paper's proofs, the chances are that the riskier paragraphs would have been at once excised. But he was otherwise engaged. And though *The Highlander* subsequently expressed its editor's 'regret' that its report of the Uig flood had 'most unfortunately been construed as reflecting injuriously on Major Fraser of Kilmuir and representing in an unfair and untrue light his treatment of his tenants', the damage had been done. Egged on by his fellow proprietors, who were understandably delighted to have been presented with such a glorious opportunity to silence both John Murdoch and his newspaper, Fraser decided to sue for £1000 damages.

There followed an acrimonious court case in Inverness sheriff court. Fraser's lawyers called a series of witnesses of whom the foremost was his factor, Alexander MacDonald. *The Highlander*, declared MacDonald, was a subversive publication. It was trying to stir up class hatred and even revolution. It was fomenting discord. It was out to discredit not only individual landowners, such as Major Fraser, but also the entire concept of private property in land. Nonsense, Murdoch replied, a little ingenuously. He was 'only labouring to bring out the state of matters in the country'.

In the end, *The Highlander* was found to have libelled the Kilmuir laird. But instead of the £1000 which he had been seeking, Fraser was awarded only £50 — together with his costs. The resulting bill came to some £85. A 'Highlander

Kilmartin River, Staffin.

Defence Fund' was got up to raise the cash required to pay it. And Murdoch's newspaper, which always existed on the brink of bankruptcy, was enabled to carry on a little longer. Not until 1881 did *The Highlander* finally succumb to the increasingly insistent demands of its many creditors. And even then it had its revenge on its former persecutor; for the paper's final issues carried the story of how crofters in Valtos and Elishader had launched the rent strike which marked the commencement of concerted resistance to William Fraser's mode of management.

*   *   *

On the agenda placed before members of the Inverness-shire police committee at their meeting on 23 September, 1884, there appeared an unprecedented item. Police constables in Skye, it was suggested, should be armed for their own protection. The police committee, it was further suggested, should immediately contact the War Office with a view to obtaining the necessary weapons. Both proposals were carried. The requisite letter was sent to London. And by the end of October, the authorities in Inverness Castle had taken delivery of 50 heavy revolvers and 1000 rounds of ammunition. Before the year was out, it was understood by all concerned, these guns might well be turned on Skye crofters.

These were unsettled and unsettling times in northern Scotland. Some three weeks before that controversial police committee meeting, the recently formed Highland Land League had held its first annual conference in Dingwall and demanded that crofters be given a statutorily guaranteed right to security of tenure as well as a share of the lands lost to crofting in the course of the clearances. And though the Land League executive had also urged their members 'to keep within the bounds of the law', it was quite obvious, by the early autumn of 1884, that this advice was not being heeded.

At Land League meetings in Tiree, for instance, it was resolved that 'the land be justly divided'. And when the island's owner, the Duke of Argyll, rejected all requests to this effect, the fences around the island's larger farms were promptly torn down.

Western Isles crofters, for their part, began simply to reoccupy the many sheep farms which owed their existence to earlier evictions and removals. 'We have put up with our grievances for a long time,' said the secretary of one Land League branch in Lewis. 'But now we venture to lay hold of a piece of our old grazings with the strong hand of the people united for their rights. Now the fence is broken down in several places and our sheep and cattle are feeding on our old possessions.'

Crofters everywhere were similarly defiant. Soon no farm fence was safe from overnight attack. Telegraph wires were cut. Boulders and other obstacles were placed on the roads in order to harass farmers, factors and landowners — the only people who could afford to travel by carriage. Rent-strikes became steadily more widespread. And the few tenants who declined to participate in them were ruthlessly intimidated. Thus one strike-breaking crofter in Kilmuir had his windows smashed, his boat wrecked and his byre set on fire.

The Highlands and Islands, it began to be asserted by southern supporters of the region's landowners, were in the grip of revolution. Throughout the Hebrides, *The Scotsman* thundered in October, 'men are taking what does not belong to them, are setting all law at defiance and are instituting a terrorism which the poor people are unable to resist. Rents are unpaid, not because the tenants cannot pay them, but because in some cases they will not and in some cases they dare not.'

It was, as they said, 'to show their detestation for the lies published in that journal' that crofters in Glendale subsequently arranged a ceremonial burning of *The Scotsman*. But other, more influential, people shared the Edinburgh newspaper's sense of outrage. That was why they had consented to the arming of the police in Skye. That was why they were prepared to countenance a police assault on the Kilmuir estate — now at the centre of the anti-landlord agitation which had so infuriated the southern political establishment.

That spring, in a sadly typical gesture, Major William Fraser had further alienated his crofting tenants by attempting to evict no less than forty of them. He had decided to expel these individuals and their families, the Kilmuir laird had announced, because their rent payments were seriously in arrears. That was true. There had, after all, been a long-running rent strike in the district. But it was also noticeable that the forty men selected for removal included all the local leaders of the Land League. Political intimidation was suspected. And when, on 31 March, a sheriff-officer arrived in Valtos with a batch of eviction orders, he was promptly attacked and driven off the estate by some 200 Land League members.

Several months later, as Inverness-shire's chief constable, Donald McHardy, was ceaselessly reminded by a police committee on which the county's landowners were well represented, no one had been charged with that particular assault. There had been no arrests, the unfortunate chief constable said repeatedly, in his turn, because Valtos, like the rest of the Kilmuir estate, had become a place where his policemen dared not go. This was an altogether deplorable state of affairs, he acknowledged. But it was nevertheless a fact. And in his, Donald McHardy's, opinion, for what it was worth, any attempt to apprehend the individuals in question would simply precipitate another riot.

And so it proved. Towards the end of October an attempt was at last made to station a superintendent and ten constables in Uig. At a spot where the road passes below that grey-painted Free Church which I mentioned a moment ago, the naturally apprehensive police contingent found themselves confronting some 200 crofters. Uig, these crofters made clear, had no need of any policemen — whereupon the constables and their officer turned round and tramped obediently back to Portree.

The Kilmuir tenants, the chief constable explained, in one of his many official communications on the subject, were in aggressive and determined

Hay-making in the evening sun, Uig.

mood. A few weeks before, he continued, some 1600 of them had met and agreed that Major Fraser would receive not one penny from them until he reduced their rents and provided them with more land. On the day following their encounter with his own men at Uig, the chief constable went on, the crofters had gathered again and, on this occasion, they had decided to occupy the land they required. 'This meeting,' ran the copy of their resolution which had come into the police's possession, 'is of the opinion that God created the land for all and not for any particular individual.'

Chief constable McHardy, for his part, expressed no view as to whether God favoured Major Fraser or, alternatively, Major Fraser's rebellious tenants. All he knew was that the approach roads to Uig, and the rest of the Kilmuir estate, were controlled by well-drilled bands of young and able-bodied crofters who were stood down only on Sundays — and then for no more than the two or three hours required to enable them to attend Gaelic service in the local Free Church.

There were reports that the Kilmuir crofters had equipped themselves with rifles as well as with the more usual clubs and pitchforks. But even if these reports were exaggerated, Donald McHardy informed his superiors in London at the beginning of November, the position was far from encouraging. The Kilmuir tenantry, he wrote, 'have for the past week been assembled in hundreds, day and night, armed with sticks for the purpose of assaulting an expected body of police. They declare that they will attack any number of constables. At present a reign of terror exists in the district and nothing short of government aid or protection for the police in restoring order and maintaining the law will suffice.'

There was then no Secretary of State for Scotland and the minister to whom Donald McHardy addressed his correspondence was Sir William Harcourt, the home secretary. Harcourt was a Liberal. And though he did not share the radical and land reforming inclinations of many of his party's backbench MPs, he was not without some sympathy for crofters. He had spent several summers yachting in the Hebrides and what he had seen there had convinced him that the problems facing Skye's proprietors were largely of these gentlemen's own making. The 'ruthless and grasping avarice' of the typical Highland laird, the home secretary observed privately, was 'unequalled anywhere'. And the Inverness-shire police were under attack, he believed, because crofters had been given good cause to regard them as agents of evicting and oppressive landlords rather than as representatives of the British crown.

It was for that reason, Sir William concluded, that despatching troops to Skye might prove to be the safest of the various choices open to him. Chief constable McHardy, as the home secretary well knew, was already training hastily recruited policemen in the use of revolvers. And if these inexperienced, but heavily armed, constables were to be deployed in Staffin, Kilmuir and Uig, where feelings were already running high and where the police were cordially loathed, then bloodshed, in the home secretary's opinion, would be virtually inevitable. On a November evening, therefore, Sir William Harcourt got to his

North-easterly gale, Bearreraig Bay.

feet in the House of Commons, then engaged in a seven-hour debate on the crofting issue, and informed MPs that, for the first time since the end of the last Jacobite Rebellion, nearly 140 years before, a military force was to be sent to Skye. It would consist, said the home secretary, of two gunboats, a troopship and 350 marines.

*   *   *

At dusk on Monday, 10 November, 1884, the gunboat HMS *Forester* slipped her moorings on the Clyde and headed downriver on the first stage of her two-day voyage to the island where she was to be joined, later that week, by a second gunboat, HMS *Banterer*, and by the troopship, HMS *Assistance*, then steaming out of Portsmouth. Awaiting *Assistance* and her 350 marines, *The Times* informed its readers, were 1200 cudgel-carrying crofters. And the 'general impression' on Skye, the paper's man in Portree reported, is that a long and tedious campaign is before us, the government having determined to crush the rebellion and prevent it spreading to other parts of the Hebrides'. If it was not quite war, then, for the press at least, it was the next best thing.

There were those who felt sorry for Skye crofters, *The Times* editorialised pompously the day before *Forester* dropped anchor off Portree. But such feelings were quite misplaced. The Kilmuir crofters had broken the law. They had refused to pay the rents to which their landlord was entitled. They had assaulted and abused the police. And if any of them should now be injured, they would have only themselves to blame. The crofters deserved, and should expect, no mercy. 'Everything must give way to the paramount necessity of restoring order.'

Restoring order, however, was proving far from easy. The contents of military despatches were being made known to island crofters by local telegraph clerks. Innkeepers and hoteliers were refusing to provide lodgings for the police who were to accompany the troops. And when the authorities, in a bid to surmount the accommodation difficulty, chartered the *Lochiel*, a steamer belonging to David MacBrayne whose shipping company was already well on its way to establishing its continuing monopoly of Hebridean ferry services, that vessel's captain and crew resigned in order to avoid any complicity in quelling crofting protest.

Amid all these upsets and alarms, only one man was seen to look well pleased. Since April 1882, when the police had first battled with island crofters at Braes, Sheriff William Ivory had wanted military intervention in Skye. Now that he had got his wish, he had taken personal command of the combined force of almost 400 soldiers and policemen which the fates, with some help from Sir William Harcourt, had put at his disposal. And on Sunday, 16 November, the day that a hastily recrewed *Lochiel* joined *Forester*, *Banterer* and *Assistance* at Portree, Ivory made known his determination to mount a massive show of strength on the Kilmuir estate.

In the early hours of Tuesday morning, then, the four ships steamed noisily into the Sound of Raasay and, skirting the basalt cliffs which marked the eastern boundary of Major Fraser's troubled possessions, set course for Rubha Hunish and Uig Bay. There the *Assistance* hove to, lowered her boats and put ashore 250 marines who, on Ivory's orders, were to march overland to Staffin, dealing rigorously with any opposition they might encounter on the way.

But no opposition was offered. A union jack had been hoisted above one croft house on the slopes above Uig. Outside another a white flag fluttered mockingly in the breeze. The Kilmuir tenantry, it was explained to the sixteen journalists accompanying the expedition, had no quarrel with the military; only with their landlord. And, indeed, scarcely any crofters were seen in the course of what one pressman called 'a ten-mile march across a bleak country'. As the troops tramped through Brogaig, Stenscholl and Staffin, however, they did not lack company. Girls appeared and were soon walking arm in arm with the sweating marines. The suggestions made in giggling Gaelic to the English soldiers, it was surmised, were not wholly proper.

Such indelicacies apart, this was not quite the civil war that had been expected. One reporter was reduced to recording that an 'old crone' had been seen to make 'derisive gestures' in the direction of the marines. And the general feeling of disillusionment was neatly summarised by the man from *The Times*. The landings at Uig and the march to Staffin, he wrote, 'were intended as an imposing military spectacle to overawe the natives. Few of these, however, were stirring, and those that were abroad seemed to be amused at, rather than intimidated by, the display. Taken as a whole, today's proceedings can only be described as an extravagant display of force, the effect of which

'Girl Margaret' at Broadford pier.

was to excite the astonishment, and mirth even, of the crofters, but not to cow them.'

Next morning *The Times* was, as usual, on the breakfast table at the London residence of Sir William Harcourt. An hour or two later, a telegram was brought to William Ivory, then back in Portree. The home secretary, the sheriff was informed, was 'somewhat surprised' that it had been thought necessary to march 250 heavily armed men through a district which, as had been amply demonstrated the day before, was entirely peaceful. There was to be no question, Harcourt reiterated, of using troops for political purposes. Certainly there was to be no question of the British army assisting island landlords to evict their crofting tenants.

That was bad news for Inverness-shire's sheriff. It was equally bad news for Major William Fraser of Kilmuir who had hoped that the military presence would facilitate his planned removal of Archibald MacDonald, a crofter at Garafad, Staffin, where he was also secretary of the local branch of the Land League.

Archibald MacDonald was then 39 and, like many other crofters at that time, he had already been evicted more than once. He had been born in a township on the other side of the hills, not far from Uig. That township had been cleared and its lands incorporated in the sheep farm of Monkstadt. His father had then been given a croft in a new township. But it, too, was cleared — 'of twenty-four families in all,' said Archibald MacDonald. 'We were scattered over the estate,' he continued, 'some to the east side, some to Kilmaluag, some to Kilmuir.' He himself had been lucky to get a holding at Garafad. But even there he had been deprived of the use of a valuable piece of hill grazing. And now Major Fraser had decided to eject him again.

That decision, however, had been taken in circumstances altogether different from those of a few years before. There were to be no more easy victories for island landlords; for William Fraser least of all.

At first, that was not obvious. The requisite legal papers were obtained readily enough and a sheriff-officer was instructed to deliver them to the Garafad crofter. But that proved impossible. On his approaching Garafad, the officer was set upon by people who pelted him mercilessly with stones, clods and, in the tactfully imprecise words of one observer, 'filth of all kinds'. Archibald MacDonald remained on his croft. And when no fewer than twenty-two of his neighbours were charged with mobbing, rioting, obstructing an officer of the law and a selection of other crimes, they simply refused to appear in court. After Garafad, Fraser of Kilmuir was obliged to abandon all attempts at eviction.

*   *   *

In the political arena, too, there was a new self-confidence, a new determination that the people of the island should at last prevail over the men who had so maltreated them. 'The crofters,' a newspaper correspondent reported from Portree on the day of the 1885 general election, 'were most enthusiastic and each approached the polling station with an air of independence which would have seemed singularly strange to any visitor who had not seen a Skye crofter during the last five years.'

That 'air of independence' brought the Highland Land League into the House of Commons. As a result of the reforming legislation which ensued, the Kilmuir estate was eventually bought by the government and its many sheep farms divided once more into crofts.

The outcome was dramatic; just how dramatic being shown by an official report on the impact made on the Kilmuir estate by a quarter century of public ownership. During that period, it was revealed, ten large farms had been eliminated. Entirely new crofts had been provided for 85 families. Another 268 crofts had been enlarged substantially. The overall area in crofting occupation had practically doubled. The area of cultivated ground had risen by almost a third. The number of thatched houses had fallen from 336 to 137. The number of slated, stone-built houses had increased from 20 to 304.

It was not denied that there might have been more profits to be made if the estate's sheep farms had been left intact. But a farm, the report's authors stated, could not, and should not, be likened to a crofting township. 'The comparison is between two entirely different things,' they wrote. 'A sheep farm is a commercial undertaking and has to be judged as such; a crofting community is a way of living and cannot be judged in terms of a profit and loss account. The people were there and insisted upon staying there. Their conditions were a reproach to the nation of which they form part, and the only way to remove that reproach was to give them the available land.'

Limestone topography, Strath.

The land that was thus restored to crofters was not always surrendered voluntarily. As can be seen by glancing at the long lists of names on any war memorial in Skye, very many islanders volunteered for military service in the First World War. And they were promised that, on their return, new crofts would be made available to them on land which the state would acquire from island lairds for that purpose. When peace came, promised one government minister in 1917, 'the land question in the Highlands' would be 'settled once and for all'. Of that the troops in the trenches need not be in any doubt. 'Everyone is agreed that the people of the Highlands must be placed in possession of the soil.'

This happy consensus, however, did not embrace Skye's proprietors. During earlier wars with revolutionary and Napoleonic France, when over 4000 islanders enlisted in the British army, island landlords had seized the opportunity to evict the absent men's families. Their successors were not about to reverse that policy now.

Not until the end of 1919, a year after the war had ground to its inglorious conclusion, did parliament pass legislation intended to redeem the pledges which had been so freely given when the carnage was at its height. And though that legislation obliged the Board of Agriculture for Scotland to purchase — compulsorily if necessary — such land as was available for settlement by homecoming servicemen, events were to demonstrate that the law, which had always been enforced vigorously when it operated to the crofting community's disadvantage, was capable of more liberal interpretation should its strict application threaten to inconvenience a landowner.

One Skye estate where surviving soldiers urgently requested crofts was Strathaird, occupying the hilly peninsula between Loch Slapin and Loch Scavaig in the south-western part of the island. In the course of the clearances, the bulk of its 14,000 acres had been divided into two enormous sheep farms. Village after village had been obliterated until there remained only a single rocky and stony crofting township, Elgol, into which there were crammed the 400 or so Strathaird people whom it had not proved feasible to transport to Australia.

For seventy years or more, Elgol's occupants had naturally coveted, as one of them remarked, 'the fine good land which our forefathers had'. And in 1920, expecting at last to obtain it, they applied for crofts at a place called Kilmarie on the much more sheltered eastern side of the peninsula. Their application, however, was unsuccessful. As a Board of Agriculture civil servant explained in confidential correspondence, the ground in question had initially been passed as suitable for settlement. But this decision had been promptly rescinded on receipt of a letter from Strathaird's owner — Walter Lyulph Johnston of Crathorne Grange, Yarm-on-Tees, Yorkshire.

The men requesting crofts at Kilmarie, their lawyer angrily informed the Scottish Office, had been 'born and brought up on the property and had, during the war, fought and bled in its defence'. That was acknowledged. But to give them what they wanted, Johnston had pointed out from Yarm-on-Tees, would detract from the outlook which he enjoyed from his Skye residence.

Bay near Achnacloich, Sleat.

And the settlement plan was accordingly dropped, as the Board of Agriculture put it, 'with a view to the preservation of the amenity of the Kilmarie Mansion House'.

On the Strathaird estate, as elsewhere in Skye, disputed farms were eventually occupied illegally and ex-servicemen jailed in consequence. Walter MacIntyre from Kilbride, then a small boy, remembers watching one such land raid in progress on a farm near his house. 'It was a spring day,' he recalls, 'and one of the landlord's labourers had come to start ploughing. He was a big, strong man, I remember. But three of the raiders had turned out and they just took the horses away from him and told him to stop. They were showing him that the land was theirs now, I suppose. And it was made theirs, in the end, though they were imprisoned first.'

It was worth running such risks to lay claim to the land that had been lost so many years before. A month or two behind bars, after all, held few terrors for young men who had seen active service on the Western Front. 'It will not frighten us though people are imprisoned for land raiding,' one Skyeman wrote defiantly to the Board of Agriculture's headquarters staff in Edinburgh. 'Better that than four years under German fire.'

* * *

Today, just across the Kilmartin River from Garafad, where crofters gathered a century ago to forestall the eviction of Archibald MacDonald, there in a big, impressive-looking building which accommodates a shop, a restaurant and a village hall. The shop is a much larger one than you expect to find in an island community. Its shelves and freezer units are well stocked. And it has something of the highly organised feel of a supermarket. That pleases its manager, Donald MacDonald, who comes from the nearby crofting township of Glasphein. 'I want this shop to be the best in Skye,' he says. That means coping with the practical problem of getting bread and milk delivered here, some 80 kilometres north of the Kyle-Kyleakin ferry, before eight o'clock in the morning. And it means cutting prices to the point where they compete with those in Portree's chain stores.

'Take the shop together with our other activities and the business is moving into profit,' Donald maintains. 'But you shouldn't assess what you see solely in terms of a balance sheet,' he adds. 'Of course, we're looking for financial success. And we're getting it. But we also exist to provide a public service. This is a social project as well as an ecomonic one.'

The company which employs Donald MacDonald to run its knitwear interests and its agricultural supplies business as well as its shop and restaurant, is called Co Chomunn Stafainn, Staffin Community Co-operative, and it is one of two dozen such enterprises in the Highlands and Islands. With a total full-time staff of about 60, and with another 200 part-timers on their books, these co-operatives have substantially boosted employment prospects. And they have also had the effect of encouraging people to participate directly in the economic development of their own districts.

Despite the availability of assistance from the Highlands and Islands Development Board, which has had a key role in the promotion of such ventures, many thousands of pounds had to be raised locally to help finance the launch of Co Chomunn Stafainn. And, in addition, about 190 people have become shareholders in the enterprise at a rate of £50 per person. 'Most of our shareholders live in the general vicinity of Staffin,' Donald MacDonald explains. 'But we have also had contributions from Inverness, Glasgow, Edinburgh and further afield. We even have one shareholder in Alice Springs, Australia.'

Donald is responsible to a management committee which is elected by these shareholders and which meets monthly to map out the co-operative's way forward. To begin with, Donald admits, the Co Chomunn concept was regarded sceptically by a number of local residents. Now, he believes, most people have been won round. The co-operative has provided badly-needed jobs. Equally significantly, it has provided a range of generally appreciated local services. This morning, Donald explains, he is wearing anorak and overalls instead of jacket and tie because he is delivering animal feed to crofters. 'The agricultural and veterinary supplies trade is now our single largest venture,' he says. 'We serve almost all the north end of the island and, though margins are low and profits hard to earn, we feel that we're doing something really worthwhile for the people we depend on.'

The telephone rings and Donald begins a Gaelic conversation with a customer. He has deliveries to make in Digg, Flodigarry and Kilmaluag. There

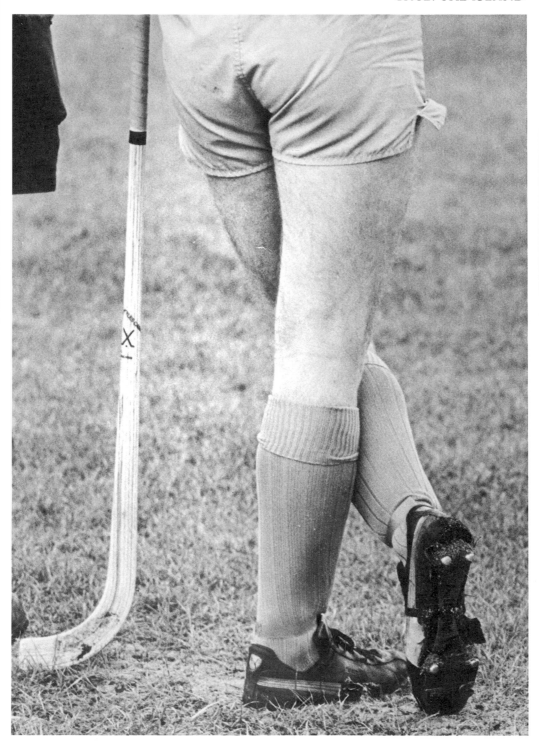

Shinty player, waiting on sidelines.

is ordering and invoicing to attend to and payments have to be made to the 30 or so people employed at home, right through the winter, producing the woollens which the co-operative sells in its craft shop during the tourist season. Plans are already being made for the next year's summer school, Airigh Shamraidh, at which youngsters from the south get a taste of life in a crofting locality. And, in between times, the village hall has to be looked after. All available bookings for the winter months have been taken by local clubs and societies, Donald remarks. Like the formation and expansion of Co Chomunn Stafainn itself, that is one more sign that Skye's crofting communities still possess the vitality that is a prerequisite for their continuance.

Checking off sheep as they are dipped.

12

ON the eastern side of Broadford Bay, in a spot exposed to the full force of Skye's frequent north-westerly gales, is one of the many crofting townships established in this southern part of Skye at the time when the second Lord Macdonald was doing his best to force his crofting tenants to supply him with the kelp that was the basis of his not inconsiderable fortune. The township's name, Waterloo, commemorates both Napoleon's final defeat and the part played in it by the 1600 men from Skye who fought, on that June day in 1815, in one or other of the many Highland detachments in the Duke of Wellington's army.

A number of these veterans were obliged eventually to settle here on crofts that none of them rated very highly. 'Our holdings are too small,' said one of Waterloo's nineteenth-century occupants, 'and they are bad. One of them is peat moss of unknown depth. Again, we can only cultivate half of our lots. At the time of year when it is wet and rainy, our beasts cannot get to the upper half of our crofts, the land is so deep and boggy. We have sometimes had to take our cattle out of the bog with ropes. Then our grazing is on soft ground also. Much of it cannot be trodden on by cattle at times.'

At the end of an exceptionally wet year, Angus MacHattie, 10 Waterloo, is inclined to endorse his Victorian predecessor's comfortless assessment of the place. Waterloo, never one of the island's better situated localities from a crofting point of view, is presently confronting more than its fair share of problems. Peats have not dried. Hay has been difficult, if not impossible, to make. There has been practically no harvest. Fodder prices are at record levels. No worthwhile emergency aid, Angus predicts, correctly as it turns out, will be forthcoming from either the British government or the European Economic Community. Some of his beasts, he says, will have to be sold because he cannot afford to keep them through the coming winter.

I ask Angus to describe a typical crofting day. There is no day that's typical, he replies. That's the trouble. But, by and large, you get up; you let out the dogs; you have your breakfast. After that, you milk the cow. You feed the inside stock. Then, at this time of year, you attend to the feeding of the outwintered beasts. And that's the better part of half a day gone already. A croft may be a very small kind of farm, Angus explains. But in the absence of the fancy equipment which the bigger operators have at their disposal, it can take just as long to deal with ten cows as with a hundred.

'Yes, I do get pretty sick of crofting at times,' Angus MacHattie admits. 'I don't like turning out in every kind of weather. I get tired of never having proper holidays. Most of all, I get fed up with having to make do with cheaply bought, clapped-out machinery that's always breaking down just when you need it most. My greatest ambition is to have a new tractor; well, not new exactly; I'd settle for one that's less than ten years old.'

So why persevere? That's not at all easy to account for, Angus answers slowly. People say it's something in your blood. And maybe people are right. In his own case, Angus explains, his family, on his mother's side, have been working land in Skye for at least eight or nine generations; latterly in Harlosh, south of Dunvegan; before that on Tarner Island in Loch Bracadale, from which the family were, at one time, evicted.

'My mother went away south to work,' Angus says. 'She got a job as a maid in a big house down there. Later she got married. And later still, she and my father, who was a policeman, got this croft in Waterloo from a distant relative. So I've been here since I was six.

'I grew up on a croft. I grew up with animals. But there was no pressure on me to become a crofter myself. In fact, there was a good deal of pressure

Angus MacHattie with son Brendan, Waterloo, Broadford.

Hallaig, Raasay.

exerted in the opposite direction, especially in school. The educational system does nothing to equip you with any practical knowledge of agriculture. Crofting, most teachers imply, is no kind of career for anyone of any talent or ambition. You'd do better to get out, they tell you. Well, I took them at their word. I went off to college. Then one night in the students union in Aberdeen, someone asked me what I was going to do with my life and it came to me that what I really wanted was to go home and work a croft. So back I came.'

That was in 1977 when Angus MacHattie was 20. He took a temporary job at the oil platform fabrication yard at Kishorn in Wester Ross. He became a postman for a year. And then, in 1978, he became a full-time crofter. Now, with ten breeding cows, 130 sheep, three goats and a pig or two, he is, he says ruefully, sufficiently successful to have obtained a much bigger overdraft than the one he had when he began.

His commitment to crofting, however, is unshaken. The future, Angus concedes, is less certain than it might be. Crofting is currently underpinned by the fact that the Common Market's agricultural policy is relatively favourable to sheep husbandry. And that might change. But there will always be opportunities for expansion, Angus MacHattie insists. And he intends to make the most of them. 'I want to increase my stock,' he says. 'I want to introduce improved grassland management methods. I want to plant trees. I want to develop the Scandinavian style of sheep housing. I want, I suppose, to show just what is possible. Just now I don't know if my own son, or others of his generation, will have any interest in crofting. But we have got to develop something that's worth handing on to them.'

There are other young men and women on the island who are equally determined to raise their families in crofting townships. But, like Angus MacHattie, they seldom find things easy. Many crofts are tenanted by people who neither work them nor live on them. And just as it is all too common for Skye people to find themselves homeless in an island with hundreds of empty houses, so it is by no means impossible for an aspiring crofter to be landless in an island where there is no scarcity of obviously neglected and semi-abandoned crofts.

Nor is officialdom, in all the many guises in which it presents itself in Skye, necessarily in sympathy with either crofters or crofting. Old prejudices die hard. And the stereotyped caricature of the idle, undeserving islander survives still in quarters where it should have been eradicated long ago. To attribute Skye's difficulties to supposed defects in the character of its inhabitants is as racist and wrong as to maintain that the undeveloped state of the African economy is a consequence of the inherent inferiority of black Africans. But for a century or more now, Skye people have had to live with jokes, cartoons and books that make them out to be boneheaded simpletons whose sole function is to make fools of themselves for the delectation of visiting southerners. And even from men employed in the public agencies which have to deal with island agriculture, I have heard no end of stories about allegedly stupid, lazy, inefficient and oversubsidised crofters whose problems, such storytellers suggest, are entirely of their own devising.

In fact, few people anywhere have had to work harder than Skye crofters to ensure the continued existence of their communities. Deprived of the bulk of their land and denied any legal rights to the few corners left to them, they had to go to war, in effect, with both their landlords and the government in order to obtain the concessions which made possible the survival of crofting. And had last century's crofters not won that particular battle, and had their more recent successors not refused to give up the desperately difficult job of making some sort of living from the land, the island would certainly have experienced much more massive depopulation than it has done.

More than fishing, more than forestry, more than tourism, more than any other form of economic activity, crofting guarantees the maintenance of viable communities in places that would otherwise be deserted. Compare the north end of Skye, where the big farms formed during the clearances were given back to crofters, with the many places in the Highlands and Islands where that did not happen. Around Staffin and Kilmuir there are still substantial numbers of people. They do not depend entirely on crofting which, for the overwhelming majority of those involved in it, remains what it has always been, a part-time occupation. But, if it were not for their crofts, these people would not be there at all and much of the island would be as empty as Rum or Mull or Morvern or the wide central straths of Sutherland where there are now practically no crofts and where, as a result, there are practically no people either.

Skye crofters certainly receive subventions from public funds. But these are not large and would be overshadowed by the expenditure incurred if crofting families were to leave the land and take up residence elsewhere. Support payments to crofters for hill sheep and cattle are a miniscule fraction of overall spending on agriculture in Britain, the greater part of which is devoted to the maintenance of cereal production. Taking into account the enormous sums that go to prop up grain prices, it is probable that the extremely wealthy occupants of one or two East Anglican farms cost the British and Western European taxpayer a good deal more than hundreds of Skye crofters. And, indeed, the total amount of public money invested annually in the island — in order to finance its schools, hospitals, roads and other services as well as its agriculture — would not pay for more than a couple of kilometres of urban motorway in the south.

Because crofters receive financial assistance to provide themselves with new homes on their crofts, crofter housing, in particular, is said widely to be heavily subsidised. The assistance in question consists of both a loan and a grant. The maxium loan, in 1986, is £10,000. All of it has to be repaid at rates which incorporate substantial interest charges. And the outright grant, made available to crofters by the Department of Agriculture for Scotland, amounts to £6500.

Given current construction costs, then, only a small proportion of a Skye crofting family's total spending on a new home is met by the state. Were such a family to abandon their croft and move to a council house in Portree or Broadford, or in Glasgow or London for that matter, the cost to the nation's taxpayers and ratepayers would be seven or eight times greater — and even

Hydro-electric power, Storr Lochs.

more than that if one takes into account the additional borrowing requirements that would be thus imposed on the country's housing authorities. And if, by way of contrast, the same family were to aspire to the purchase of a bungalow in a southern suburb, then the tax relief which would be allowable on their mortgage payments, would add up to more than that £6500 grant within no more than two or three years.

In public expenditure terms, therefore, a house on an island croft costs very much less than any other type of accommodation. And since the typical Skye crofter is himself a taxpayer, he is not so much benefiting from a housing subsidy as helping to finance the altogether larger subsidies enjoyed by other people — his own critics, no doubt, among them.

And what is true of financial aid for croft houses is also true of public spending on crofting agriculture. Most such spending takes the form of the so-called Hill Livestock Compensatory Allowances paid to all farmers and smallholders living in the European Economic Community's more remote and marginal localities. And in most Common Market countries these HLCAs, as they are called, are graded in such a way as to ensure that the man with only a small flock or herd gets a much higher rate per animal than the bigger and more affluent operator. Smaller agricultural enterprises are thus kept in profit and the overall rural population is consequently maintained at a comparatively high level.

But in the United Kingdom, where agricultural policy is dictated very largely by the nation's more substantial farmers and landowners, there is a very different policy. The Skye crofter with two or three dozen breeding ewes gets exactly the same payment on each sheep as the laird whose flocks are numbered in thousands. Such a system, by favouring the bigger unit at the expense of the smallholding, actually makes it more, rather than less, likely that crofters will go out of business. It is, then, scarcely in accord with the stated European Community objective of keeping as many people as possible on the land in places like Skye. But since British governments, now as in the past, are inclined to pay more attention to landlords and to larger farmers than to crofters, no great change is probable. Island proprietors will go on being subsidised at the expense of island crofters.

Crofting will endure, however. Now that British and European agricultural policy — long directed towards increased output, greater mechanisation and ever more extensive farms — is coming unstuck in a welter of grain and beef and butter mountains, there is a new and welcome emphasis on the need to combine farming with other activities in order to sustain worthwhile rural populations. Farmers must diversify, we are told. They must look to the land for only one part of their revenue. They must develop alternative sources of revenue. And that, of course, is what crofters have been doing successfully for very many years.

Skye crofters once made kelp. Now they fish, take in tourists, drive lorries, run garages and shops, teach, nurse, work in the offshore oil industry, lecture, write, broadcast, make transducers, manage building firms and do much else. New information technologies and advances in electronic communications

Braes and Glamaig from Raasay.

techniques will permit further development and make it possible to do more widely what is done already in one or two instances: run a national, or even international, business from a crofting village.

These things will happen anyway. They could be made to happen more quickly with the appropriate assistance; just as, given a little imagination on the part of government, crofters could become fish farmers and foresters in their own right; just as, with the necessary encouragement, the same crofters could take full responsibility for the management of the land on which they live.

Skye's crofting communities, then, should not be presented to visitors as quaint leftovers from another age. Nor should island crofters be treated as some sort of rare and threatened species deserving of protection. Instead, they should simply be accorded the right to make the most of the opportunity now available to them; the opportunity to demonstrate that crofting can be the basis of an attractive way of living in both this century and the next.

* * *

'During the time I was away at college,' Angus MacHattie says, 'I used to feel my morale plummet every time I left the island. Then, coming back, down through Glen Shiel, towards Loch Duich and Dornie, I'd feel my spirits lift again. It was good to be getting home, I suppose, good to be getting back where

I belong. I don't know how you evaluate that sort of thing. But, yes, the island means a lot to me. I think it means a lot to all Skye people.'

That love of Skye has been there for a long time. But it was long expended hopelessly on lamenting the need to emigrate to other parts of the world; because of the clearances; because of poverty; because of lack of land; because of the impossibility of obtaining work. Now that same sentiment is at last being channelled into constructive action here on the island. Angus MacHattie, running his own croft and representing the island on the executive council of Aonachd nan Chroitearan, the recently created Scottish Crofters Union, is one example of the new determination to make a go of things at home. Also indicative of changed attitudes is Aonachd nan Chroitearan itself. With more members than any crofting organisation since the Highland Land League of the 1880s, the Crofters Union, which has its headquarters in Broadford, reflects the emergence of an overdue political aggressiveness on the part of island communities.

The odds against these communities being allowed to shape their own destinies are quite overwhelming. The island is remote from the centres of national life. Its influence on government, as only a small part of one of over 600 British parliamentary constituencies, is virtually nil. Its land and its resources are still controlled, for the most part, by outsiders. And for every Skye person who speaks the island's ancient and imperilled language, there are, in the rest of the world, almost a quarter of a million people who speak English.

But there is also cause for optimism; more cause than at any time in the last hundred years. Skye's population, which fell steadily in each of the thirteen decades following the great famine of the 1840s, has finally begun to rise. In the island's Gaelic playgroups and in its Gaelic College, in its local history societies and in its support for ventures like Co Chomunn Stafainn, I believe, there is to be discerned some sign of what has for far too long been lacking: a pride in Skye, its culture and its heritage; a conviction that there is something here that is well worth maintaining.

'And when I am in my coffin,' predicted *Mairi Mhor nan Oran*, 'my words will be as a prophecy. And there will return the stock of the tenantry who were driven over the sea. And the gentry will be routed, as they, the crofters, were. Deer and sheep will be wheeled away and the glens will be tilled. There will be a time of sowing and of reaping; a time of reward for the robbers. And the cold, ruined stances of houses will be built on by our kinsmen.' Today, though big Mary MacPherson's vision remains a long, long way from realisation, it is less evidently the delusion that once it must have seemed.

* * *

On the morning of my leaving Skye, the sun first illuminates the tops of Uchd Mor and Cnoc an t-Sithein at just after nine o'clock. As the light moves slowly down the slope, it catches the withered stems of the deer grass where they project from the snow and, as the hillside takes on a faintly orange glow in consequence, the landscape suddenly seems warmer. But that is an illusion.

Bend in the River Drynoch, at Drynoch.

Outside the air is still and brittle in the frost. This morning there was no water from the taps. And as I go to fill a kettle and a bucket from the ice-fringed burn on the far side of the road, the dried-out snow creaks softly beneath my boots.

Two members of the Skye Mountain Rescue Team: Ewen MacKinnon and John MacLeod.

Sheep shearing, Drynoch.

The sun is just above the Cuillins now. I blot it out with one hand and look again at that long row of peaks: Sgurr nan Gillean, Bruach na Frithe, Sgurr na Bairnich, Sgurr an Fheadain, Sgurr a' Mhadaidh, Sgurr Thuilm, Sgurr a' Ghreadhaidh, Sgurr nan Gobhar, Sgurr na Banachdich. Because of the sun's glow behind them, they seem dark and one-dimensional; a frieze of sharp and sawtoothed summits; the sort of mountains a child might put in her painting.

Inside again, I fold away my ordnance survey maps. I gather up the books from the table and the window sill: Sorley MacLean's collected poetry; Christian Watt's autobiography with its mention of Kate MacLeod from Suisnish; Samuel Johnson's *Journey to the Western Islands*; the bulky volume containing the hundreds of pages of closely printed evidence taken by the royal commission of 1883 from islanders like Angus Stewart and John MacPherson.

I pack the notebooks filled with scribbled summaries of conversations that took place on crofts, in cars, in caravans, in trains, in houses, in pubs; notebooks which also have blurred and wrinkled pages showing where I tried to make some immediate record, in the rain, of my impressions of the localities mentioned in this book. And, finally, I gather up the elements of this book itself; still handwritten, still with scorings-out, additions and insertions and subtractions. The thing is not yet, here and there, the way I think it ought to be. But, for the moment, it will have to do.

In the afternoon, the sky is duller. There is ice on the road where it crosses Allt na Guile. There is more ice in Glen Drynoch and the lochans on the right-hand side near Sligachan are frozen right across.

Wedged between hills that are all greys and whites, the sea seems strangely colourless. There is only a light breeze on the water. But the snow is being lifted from the top of Glamaig by the wind. And the almost yellowish clouds towards Raasay warn of the imminent onset of a squall.

I stop at Bruach nam Bo and watch the storm's advancing edge come up Loch Ainort. The hills have already vanished. Soon the floating wooden cages at the salmon farm in the loch's north-western corner are no longer visible. A sudden burst of hail clatters on the car. And then the snow comes swirling thickly, blowing across the ground and quickly covering the road.

At Broadford, though it is barely after three, the street lights have come on in the growing darkness. Big, heavy flakes are eddying around them. And I agree with the man who gives me petrol that it is going to be a right rough night.

But there we are both wrong. Across the ferry, not far beyond Kyle of Lochalsh, I pause for a minute or two in a roadside layby. The snow has stopped. The clouds have cleared away. The evening has all the noiselessness that goes with a deep frost. I stand there in the cold and I look across Loch Alsh to Beinn na Caillich and Sgurr na Coinnich, their bulky shapes glinting dimly in the starlight. There is no message there. On the issues with which this book has been primarily concerned, the island itself is strictly neutral. Skye's future will be entirely what we make of it.